TOKUGAWA IEYASU

LEADERSHIP ▪ STRATEGY ▪ CONFLICT

STEPHEN TURNBULL ▪ ILLUSTRATED BY GIUSEPPE RAVA

First published in 2012 by Osprey Publishing
Midland House, West Way, Botley, Oxford OX2 0PH, UK
44-02 23rd St, Suite 219, Long Island City, NY 11101, USA

E-mail: info@ospreypublishing.com

© 2012 Osprey Publishing Limited

Osprey Publishing is part of the Osprey Group

Print ISBN: 978 1 84908 574 8
PDF e-book ISBN: 978 1 84908 575 5
EPUB e-book ISBN: 978 1 78096 446 1

Editorial by Ilios Publishing Ltd, Oxford, UK (www.iliospublishing.com)
Cartography: Mapping Specialists Ltd.
Page layouts by Myriam Bell Design, UK
Index by Sandra Shotter
Originated by PDQ Digital Media Solutions
Printed in China through Worldprint Ltd

12 13 14 15 16   10 9 8 7 6 5 4 3 2 1

A CIP catalogue record for this book is available from the British Library.

www.ospreypublishing.com

Dedication

To my grandson Jacob Stephen Turnbull, born 1 November 2011

Artist's note

Readers may care to note that the original paintings from which the colour plates in this book were prepared are available for private sale. All reproduction copyright whatsoever is retained by the Publishers. All enquiries should be addressed to:

Giuseppe Rava, via Vorgotto 17, 48018 FAENZA (RA), Italy
Email: info@g-rava.it
Website: www.g-rava.it

The Publishers regret that they can enter into no correspondence upon this matter.

Editor's note

All images are from the author's collection

The Woodland Trust

Osprey Publishing are supporting the Woodland Trust, the UK's leading woodland conservation charity, by funding the dedication of trees.

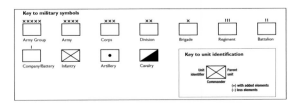

CONTENTS

INTRODUCTION

Tokugawa Ieyasu (1542–1616) is the pivotal figure of early modern Japan. He was the military leader who completed the reunification of Japan after more than a century of civil war and then restored for himself the central governing position of shogun (effectively the military dictator) following his victory at Sekigahara in 1600, one of the most decisive battles in Japanese history. Yet his triumph did more than bring peace to Japan; it placed his family in a position of dominance that they were to enjoy for two and a half centuries until the emergence of modern Japan. All this was achieved through the generalship and statesmanship of a truly great commander.

The Age of Warring States

In this portrait scroll the great commander Tokugawa Ieyasu is shown in later life as the accomplished and dignified courtier and statesman that he became.

Ieyasu's last battle at Osaka in 1615, when the final objectors to his rule were eliminated, brought to a close the period of strife into which he had been born seven decades earlier. It was an age when the particular circumstances of his own family echoed the situation in Japan as a whole. This era was Japan's *Sengoku Jidai*, the 'Age of Warring States', a title borrowed from Ancient Chinese history that was to be applied to the period of about a century and a half after 1467 when Japanese society was characterized by numerous wars between rival daimyo (warlords). Tokugawa Ieyasu would eventually bring this time of civil wars to an end, but none could have foreseen such a destiny for the baby son born to a minor provincial warrior called Matsudaira Hirotada (1526–49), whose personal situation was anything but auspicious.

Ieyasu's father was one of many local warlords whose recent ancestors had taken advantage of the earlier collapse in central authority to set up petty kingdoms of their own. The year 1467 had seen a major upheaval in Japanese history, because prior to that date local government had been exercised through a deputy appointed by the shogun, the dictator who ruled from the imperial capital city of Kyoto. There had been shoguns for almost two centuries, although the ancient title had originally referred only to a superlative warrior who was given a temporary commission to fight the enemies of the emperor of Japan. These temporary shoguns were chosen from landowners whose personal wealth had allowed them to create a private army of 'men who served', i.e. 'samurai'. The power and influence of these local 'barons' was tolerated so long as the targets of their aggression were the enemies of the throne, and for many years the system worked, proving to successive emperors that it was better to rely on hiring private armies than to use the much-disliked alternative of conscription. So samurai armies put down rebels in the north-east of Japan and quelled pirates in the south-west, and proved very useful in guarding the imperial capital. The rewards were generous, and the samurai leaders grew richer.

In 1156, however, a serious development occurred when the two most powerful samurai families took sides in a conflict over the claims of rival candidates for emperor. The opponents did not then divide along clan lines, but that was to happen during a further conflict in 1161, and the reprisals taken afterwards made a major clash between them more certain. The result was a fiercely contested civil war known to history as the Gempei War. It began in 1180 with an uprising by the Minamoto family in the name of

an alternative candidate in another dispute over the imperial succession. Their ire was directed against rivals from the Taira family, who had married into the imperial line and were now trying to control affairs from within the court bureaucracy. The two clans had been heavily involved in the disputes of 1156 and 1161, but the Gempei War of 1180 to 1185 was to result in the complete elimination of the Taira as a political and military force. The final battle, fought at sea off the beach of Dan no Ura near the modern city of Shimonoseki in Yamaguchi Prefecture, was one of the most decisive battles of Japanese history, where the sea flowed red from the blood of the slain and the dye from the flags of the vanquished Taira. The infant emperor Antoku, whose grandfather was a Taira, died during the battle, so it was the Minamoto imperial nominee who became the new emperor.

The victorious Minamoto then took steps to ensure their family's mastery of the governance of Japan and with it the total dominance of the samurai class over the bureaucracy of the imperial court. Instead of ruling behind the scenes as the Taira had done, the Minamoto revived the tradition of

This *kakemono* (hanging scroll) shows Tokugawa Ieyasu sitting on his camp stool on a battlefield. His *jinbaori* (surcoat) carries the *mon* (badge) of the Tokugawa, while behind him stands one of his best-known helmets bearing a gold fern *maedate* (frontlet). Above flies his gold fan standard. This is sometimes depicted with a red rising sun on it, but the extant specimen is plain gold.

appointing someone as shogun. The difference now was that the commission was to be a permanent appointment rather than a temporary one. Japan's first permanent shogun, Minamoto Yoritomo (1147–99), was therefore appointed in 1192. It was always intended that the position of shogun should stay within the Minamoto family, and, allowing for some creative genealogy, it did until 1868 when the last shogun handed back the commission to the new Meiji emperor as Japan prepared to enter the modern age. The surname of this last shogun was Tokugawa, because he was a descendant of Tokugawa Ieyasu, the subject of this book, who revived the shogunate in 1603 following a hiatus when Japan was ruled by Oda Nobunaga (1534–82) and Toyotomi Hideyoshi (1536–98). Neither of these men possessed the appropriate lineage to become shogun. Only the Tokugawa, with their proof of descent from the Minamoto, could revive that institution.

The Matsudaira family

Tokugawa Ieyasu was the son of a minor daimyo of Mikawa Province (the eastern half of modern Aichi Prefecture) called Matsudaira Hirotada. Since 1467, warlords like Ieyasu's father had fought one another for local influence rather than having it delegated to them by a now virtually powerless shogun. Thus it was that the future shogun Tokugawa Ieyasu was born into relative obscurity in Mikawa, through which ran the Tokaido Road, Japan's main means of communication with the east of the country from Kyoto. His father Matsudaira Hirotada was to spend much of his short life defending this patch of territory against predatory neighbours in a manner typical of any Sengoku warrior. Hirotada's main enemy was Oda Nobuhide (d. 1549), who was based across the provincial border in Owari (the western half of modern Aichi Prefecture). Nobuhide was the father of Oda Nobunaga the first of the three unifiers of Japan.

This statue of Tokugawa Ieyasu stands in the grounds of his castle of Okazaki. This was the chief castle of the Matsudaira, but Ieyasu spent little time there during his youth owing to his forced residence at Sumpu.

Matsudaira Hirotada had led a precarious existence since childhood, and had been only ten years old when he had lost his own father Matsudaira Kiyoyasu in a tragic incident involving Abe Sadayoshi, a hereditary retainer of the Matsudaira, who had come under suspicion of treason. Surrounded by his accusers Abe protested his innocence, but at that moment his horse became restless. Kiyoyasu called out for the horse to be secured, but Abe Yashichi, the son of Sadayoshi, heard the shouts and thought that Kiyoyasu had given an order for his father to be apprehended, not the horse, so he immediately drew his sword and killed Kiyoyasu. The incident fortunately did not create any animosity towards his father, who continued to stay loyal to the memory of Kiyotada by taking responsibility for the welfare of his heir Hirotada, who was now an orphan of ten years old.

One of the best ways of safeguarding the future of the Matsudaira house was for them to seek an alliance with a powerful neighbour. To reach any understanding with their long-standing enemy Oda Nobuhide was out of the question, but on the other side of Mikawa Province lay the well-established territory of the powerful Imagawa Yoshimoto (1519–60), who responded positively to Abe Sadayoshi's request for help. The Matsudaira were now more secure, and in 1541 Hirotada married the daughter of his former enemy Mizuno Tadamasa, lord of the castle of Kariya in Mikawa. The following year his wife gave birth to their first child at the age of 15, the future Tokugawa Ieyasu, in Hirotada's capital of Okazaki. Meanwhile the Matsudaira were heavily involved in wars on behalf of the Imagawa, who expected military service for their support. Four months before Ieyasu was born Hirotada fought the Oda at the first battle of Azukizaka. By way of retaliation, Oda Nobuhide was to be found attacking Hirotada's castle of Ueno only two days before the 17-year-old Hirotada became the father of a future shogun.

THE EARLY YEARS

The infant name given to the new arrival in the Matsudaira family was Takechiyo, a poetic expression which indicated his parents' hopes that he would enjoy the longevity of 'a thousand ages like the bamboo'. This was an optimistic wish for someone born during the Sengoku Period, because not only was there war going on all around him, his own family was falling apart. First Hirotada's uncle, Matsudaira Nobutaka, went over to the side of Oda Nobuhide. This gave Nobuhide the confidence to attack Okazaki in 1543. Then Hirotada's father-in-law died, and his heir Mizuno Nobutomo rediscovered his former enmity against the Matsudaira and declared his support for Oda Nobuhide as well. As his wife's family were now ranged against him, Hirotada felt duty-bound to divorce her and send her back to her ancestral family, so she was escorted away from her baby son when he was only one year old. Hirotada soon took a second wife who was eventually to bear him further children, but young Takechiyo had now lost his mother.

It was not long before Oda Nobuhide made another attack on Okazaki, which he perceived to be weaker as a result of the confusion within the Matsudaira household. He was probably right, because Hirotada was forced to turn to his ally Imagawa Yoshimoto for further military intervention. It was willingly given, but there were now strict conditions, one of which was that the child Takechiyo should be handed over to the Imagawa as a hostage for good behaviour, a not uncommon practice. The old Matsudaira retainers felt insulted at the demand and it pained Hirotada to have to send away his only son, but he had little choice other than to agree. So Takechiyo

As a boy Tokugawa Ieyasu was known as Takechiyo and spent most of his young life as a hostage, first of the Oda and then of the Imagawa in their capital of Sumpu (modern Shizuoka), where this cartoon-like statue of Takechiyo has recently been erected.

set off for Imagawa's castle of Sumpu (modern Shizuoka City, Shizuoka Prefecture) under armed guard, but then tragedy struck, because while they were still crossing Mikawa Province their party was intercepted by Oda Nobuhide's men, who kidnapped Takechiyo and bundled him off to Owari. The inevitable message followed: that Takechiyo would be put to death if Hirotada did not surrender Okazaki Castle.

Oda Nobuhide was not expecting the reply he received from Matsudaira Hirotada: that he might as well kill Takechiyo as he had been sent as a hostage to the Imagawa anyway and that his failure to arrive was no fault of the Matsudaira family. Indeed, stated Hirotada, his alliance with the Imagawa might even be strengthened by Takechiyo's death when Imagawa realized that Hirotada was willing to sacrifice his only son. Bluff or not, this defiant reply resulted in no harm being done to Takechiyo, who was kept as a hostage of the Oda for the next three years. His mother, who had since remarried, was not far away, and even though she was not allowed to see her son she was able to keep in touch with him. Meanwhile Matsudaira Hirotada kept on fighting for himself and for the cause of the Imagawa. He and Oda Nobuhide clashed at Anjo Castle, and then Hirotada survived an assassination attempt. Finally, after another battle in 1549 where Hirotada got the better of Oda Nobuhide, both these bitter rivals died from disease within a short time of each other.

The death of Nobuhide caused more problems for the house of Oda than the death of Hirotada did for the house of Matsudaira, because a dispute began between Nobuhide's sons that was eventually to result in the dominance of the Oda by the famous Nobunaga. Taking advantage of the confusion the Imagawa went to war against them, and one of these actions resulted in an important deal. Seeing that they had Oda Nobunaga at their mercy, the Imagawa agreed not to press home their attack if he released the hostage Takechiyo. This Nobunaga agreed to do, and Takechiyo, by then eight years old, returned to Okazaki. He was not allowed to stay there any longer than the time it took him to perform ancestral rites for his father, because he was soon taken off to Sumpu, the destination intended for him before his kidnapping. So the future leader of the family moved from one hostage situation to another, but as the Matsudaira were allied with the Imagawa rather than fighting them his situation was much improved

This upper-body detail from a hanging scroll in Mito, the seat of one of the most important branches of the Tokugawa family, shows Tokugawa Ieyasu in an elaborate helmet ornamented with a golden dragon.

compared to his previous incarceration. Takechiyo had playmates and companions in Sumpu Castle, some of whom were to become his most loyal companions in adulthood. One of them, Torii Mototada, was virtually to sacrifice his own life for Ieyasu in 1600.

Ieyasu performed his *gembuku* (manhood ceremony) at the age of 15. Imagawa Yoshimoto presided and gave the former Takechiyo the adult name of Matsudaira Motonobu. Not long afterwards he was given permission to visit Okazaki. He was, after all, the head of the Matsudaira family, but owing to his two episodes as a hostage his followers had seen precious little of him since his birth and were firmly under the control of Imagawa Yoshimoto. Consequently Motonobu's return to pay his respects to the tomb of his father Matsudaira Hirotada and to receive the homage of his retainers was a moving event for all concerned. He was received at Okazaki by the *karo* (senior retainer) of the Matsudaira, Torii Tadayoshi, father of Mototada. He showed Motonobu round the place that was rightfully his, and drew his attention in particular to the care Tadayoshi had taken with the stores of rice and money that he kept there away from the prying eyes of their Imagawa overlords.

Motonobu was not able to stay long at Okazaki, and, under the terms of the hostage agreement, he returned without protest to Sumpu. The wars between the Oda were still continuing and the Matsudaira were taking the brunt of the fighting, but Sumpu was never remotely threatened and it was there in 1557 that Motonobu got married. He wed, almost inevitably, a relative of Imagawa Yoshimoto, the daughter of Sekiguchi Chikanaga. At the same time he changed his name again to Motoyasu, taking the second character from his late grandfather Kiyoyasu, whom he greatly admired. With his true family having acknowledged him, and safely married into the Imagawa family, he could now be trusted to move forward one more stage in his service to Imagawa Yoshimoto. It was time for the future Tokugawa Ieyasu to fight his first battle.

Opposite Ieyasu's mother was only 15 when she gave birth to the future shogun. When her family turned against the Matsudaira her husband divorced her and sent her back to her own family. This embroidery of her is in Shizuoka.

The partly restored castle of Sumpu (modern Shizuoka) enthusiastically celebrates its link with Tokugawa Ieyasu, who was a hostage there under the Imagawa. In the museum there is this excellent reproduction of Ieyasu's gold-lacquered armour, of which the original is in the Kunozan Shrine Museum. He is believed to have worn this armour during his early campaigns.

THE MILITARY LIFE

We may assume that during his years as a youth at Sumpu, Tokugawa Ieyasu became proficient in the martial arts, the most vital set of accomplishments for anyone who belonged to Japan's military class. The world of art, religion and politics would also not have been neglected, and indeed Sumpu was an excellent place to imbibe all these skills because Imagawa Yoshimoto maintained an elegant capital there that was renowned as a 'little Kyoto'. He could afford to indulge in such passions because his domain was defended by a loyal army that tended to be successful in battle as long as Imagawa Yoshimoto was not actually leading it in person.

Ieyasu's first battles

Matsudaira Motoyasu went into battle for the first time in 1558. A certain Suzuki Shigeteru had betrayed the Imagawa by handing over his castle of Terabe in Western Mikawa to Oda Nobunaga. This was nominally Motoyasu's own territory, so he was sent by Imagawa Yoshimoto to recapture his own fortress. He led an army of Matsudaira retainers out of Okazaki Castle, an event they must have eagerly anticipated for years. At Terabe Castle we see the young Ieyasu in action for the first time, and this is not the picture of a great general sitting on a camp stool at the rear of his troops that Ieyasu was later to present. Instead he led the attack in person as a brave yet very cool commander. He first attacked and burned several of the outer defences of Terabe, but fearing that he might be taken in the rear he set fire to the main castle and withdrew. Just as he had anticipated, Oda Nobunaga arrived to attack him from behind, but Motoyasu was ready for him and rearranged his army with great rapidity so that he drove Nobunaga away. After this he returned to Sumpu to be congratulated and rewarded, having given an excellent indication of his skills as a commander.

In 1559 Ieyasu again demonstrated his military acumen by shepherding a packhorse column into Odaka Castle under the noses of Oda Nobunaga's army. Odaka was the only one of five disputed frontier forts not in Nobunaga's hands, and it desperately needed supplies. Ieyasu launched diversionary attacks against two of the other forts, at which the garrisons of the remaining two came out to their assistance. Ieyasu's supply column was waiting in readiness, and as soon as the two nearest forts were denuded of troops Ieyasu calmly marched into Odaka. This was a very different action from the fight at Terabe and showed the breadth of Ieyasu's talents, not the least of which was intelligence.

In 1560 Ieyasu went to war on behalf of the Imagawa once again in the campaign that ended with the tragedy of the battle of Okehazama. Imagawa Yoshimoto had invaded Owari Province and outnumbered Oda Nobunaga by a vast degree. Ieyasu gave a very good account of himself during the early successful stages by capturing one of Nobunaga's castles. This was Marune, which Ieyasu attacked vigorously before withdrawing to prepared positions to await a counterattack. When the Oda defenders sallied out they were caught in a furious

In the scene from *Ehon Toyotomi Kunkoki*, an illustrated life of Toyotomi Hideyoshi, we see the defeat of Sakuma Daigaku Morishige at the hands of Tokugawa Ieyasu during Ieyasu's capture of the fortress of Marune in 1560. The taking of Marune was followed shortly afterwards by the debacle of the battle of Okehazama.

Opposite:
1. Ieyasu spends most of his childhood as a hostage of the Imagawa in Sumpu.
2. Ieyasu fights his first battle at Terabe in 1558.
3. Ieyasu provisions Odaka Castle in 1559.
4. In 1560, having captured Marune, Ieyasu rests at Odaka and avoids the battle of Okehazama.
5. In a bold raid on Kaminojo in 1562 Ieyasu takes hostages for exchange.
6. Taking possession of Okazaki, Ieyasu fights the Ikko-ikki at Azukizaka in 1564.
7. After defeating Imagawa Ujizane at Kakegawa, Ieyasu moves his capital to Hamamatsu in 1570.

Ieyasu's wars on behalf of the Imagawa and the consolidation of his independent status, 1558–70

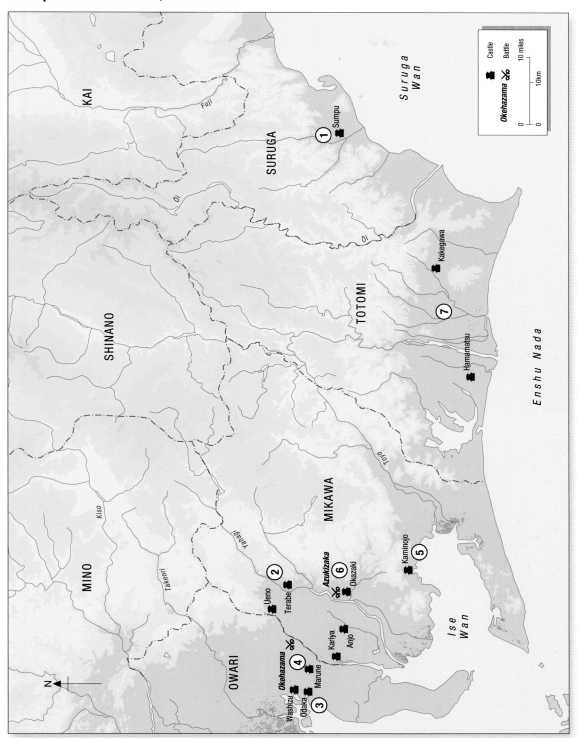

barrage of arrows and musket balls and their commander was killed. Ieyasu's army then pursued them and the castle fell.

Ieyasu was then ordered to move into Odaka Castle to rest his men and horses while Yoshimoto began a head-viewing ceremony. It was an order that probably saved Ieyasu's life, because Yoshimoto chose to rest at a place in the open air called Okehazama, a narrow wooded gorge. It was territory that his enemy Oda Nobunaga knew well, and it provided the perfect opportunity for a surprise attack. Nobunaga led 3,000 men on a circular route through the wooded hills to drop down beside Okehazama from the north. As Nobunaga's men drew silently near a terrific thunderstorm began, which cloaked their final movements as Imagawa's men huddled under trees from the torrential rain. When the clouds blew away the Oda troops poured into the gorge. The Imagawa samurai were so unprepared for an attack that they fled in all directions, leaving Yoshimoto's *maku* (curtained field headquarters) quite unprotected. Imagawa Yoshimoto had so little knowledge of what was going on that

Imagawa Yoshimoto controlled the Matsudaira family for many years. Tokugawa Ieyasu was his hostage for almost his entire childhood and then went on to fight for Yoshimoto until the latter's death in 1560. The Imagawa army was usually successful as long as Yoshimoto was not leading it in person, as was to be demonstrated by the disaster at Okehazama.

he drew the conclusion that a drunken fight had broken out among his men, and seeing an angry-looking samurai running towards him barked out an order for the man to return to his post. He only realized that it was one of Nobunaga's men when the samurai aimed a spear-thrust at him, but by then it was too late. He drew his sword and cut through the shaft of the spear, but before he could do any more a second samurai grabbed him and lopped off his head. All but two senior officers of the defeated Imagawa army were killed.

Ieyasu's fight for Mikawa

The death of Imagawa Yoshimoto and Ieyasu's fortuitous absence from the scene meant that he now had the opportunity to assert his independence, so, when the defeated Imagawa men abandoned Okazaki for the safety of Sumpu, Ieyasu marched into the castle and reclaimed his ancestral inheritance. He then began to set up an alliance with the victorious Oda Nobunaga, a fruitful partnership that was to last until the latter's death in 1582. This was done in secret at first because Imagawa Ujizane, heir to the unfortunate Yoshimoto, held a number of hostages from Ieyasu's family, including his wife and son, whose throats would surely be cut at the least indication of a change of allegiance. Yet once again Ieyasu's boldness and calculating mind came together to solve the problem in one dramatic stroke in the year 1562, the same year that Motoyasu changed his name to the better-known Ieyasu. The Imagawa's western outpost was a castle called Kaminojo, held for them by a certain Udono Nagamochi. It promised to be a useful prize for the Oda, and if Ieyasu was able to capture it on Nobunaga's behalf any hostages taken from Kaminojo could be exchanged for Ieyasu's own family. It would of course have to be done quickly before the news got out and Imagawa had a chance to murder Ieyasu's relatives, so he hired men to carry out a classic *ninja* raid under cover of darkness. The raiding party deliberately made as little sound as possible while they ran around killing, so that the defenders thought they were traitors from within the garrison. The *ninja* were also dressed like the defenders, thereby causing more confusion, and as they spread out they communicated with one another using a password. Two hundred of the Udono garrison were burned to death in the conflagration that followed, but this was of less importance to Ieyasu than the priceless reward of Udono's two sons as hostages, whom Ieyasu exchanged for his own family.

Between 1563 and 1564 Ieyasu took on some very different opponents. Even though the underlying trend during the Age of Warring States was for daimyo to grow in strength by overcoming rivals who would pledge vows of vassaldom and join an expanding *gundan* (war band), an important exception lay with the voluntary combination of small landowners into *ikki* (leagues). The strongest *ikki* were those that shared a common religious belief, and Mikawa Province was an important centre for the Ikko-ikki (the Single-Minded League) who fielded armies of believers from the Buddhist Jodo Shinshu (True Pure Land) sect. One characteristic shared by the Ikko-ikki members in Mikawa was a certain amount of divided loyalty between the demands of their faith and the prospect of fighting for a successful commander such as Tokugawa Ieyasu. Using the same combination of diplomacy and military acumen that was to be a hallmark of his later career, Ieyasu exploited this factor. So Honda Tadakatsu, the head of the main branch of the Honda family, abandoned the True Pure Land for the Pure Land (Ieyasu's Buddhist sect of choice), and went on to serve under Ieyasu's standard in all his future battles. By contrast, Honda Masanobu from the junior branch of the family chose to fight for the Ikk -ikki and only submitted to Ieyasu after their defeat. Nevertheless he was to rise to prominence in later life as one of Ieyasu's closest advisers. Further cunning came with a peace agreement whereby the temples of the Ikko-ikki were to be returned to their natural state, which Ieyasu interpreted as meaning green fields with no buildings left standing.

A diorama formerly in Okazaki Castle showing Ieyasu's samurai attacking a Jodo Shinshu temple in Mikawa Province, which is being stoutly defended by members of the Ikko-ikki.

The free hand that Ieyasu gave himself during the second battle of Azukizaka in 1564, which was fought against the Mikawa Ikko-ikki, echoed his close involvement in leadership during the siege of Terabe, but also shows an element of recklessness in the heat of battle. We know from accounts of the fighting that Ieyasu was personally engaged in horseman-to-horseman spear combat, and, even though as the commander loyal bodyguards surrounded him, he caused them considerable alarm. Once again the conflict of loyalties on the part of Ikko-ikki members played a part in Ieyasu's survival, because some would not press home their attack against their nominal lord whom they clearly admired. Even so, on returning home to Okazaki Castle Ieyasu stripped off his armour and two spent bullets fell out of his shirt.

By now almost all of Mikawa Province was his. Imagawa Ujizane was the only obstacle left, and the final districts of Mikawa passed to Ieyasu after the successful capture of Ujizane's Yoshida Castle (modern Toyohashi). It was soon time for a final push against Ujizane's remaining provinces so that Ieyasu could take over from his former overlord. For this Ieyasu made an alliance with Takeda Shingen, the great daimyo of Kai Province (modern Yamanashi Prefecture), whereby Ieyasu would receive Totomi Province and Shingen would acquire Suruga from the former Imagawa domains. When Shingen advanced into Suruga, Ujizane fled from Sumpu and took refuge in Kakegawa, thereby abandoning one of his provinces to the Takeda. Ieyasu then besieged him in Kakegawa, and suggested that if Ujizane gave him Totomi he would

Tokugawa Ieyasu leads the charge at the second battle of Azukizaka, 1564

Ieyasu was a young general recently freed from his obligations to the Imagawa. He had reclaimed his inheritance of Mikawa Province and was determined to crush all his remaining opponents. At Azukizaka he took on the army of the Mikawa Ikko-ikki, the Buddhist fanatics of the Jodo Shinshu sect. Many samurai fought for the Ikko-ikki in spite of their supposed vassal status to the Matsudaira family. Accompanying Ieyasu were warrior monks from his own Buddhist sect of Jodo.

As a young general, Ieyasu believed in leading from the front, and heads up the advance of his followers in a vigorous charge through the Ikko-ikki lines. Although we do not know for certain which design of armour Ieyasu wore at any of his battles, this gold-lacquered armour laced in green, which is preserved at the Kunozan Toshogu Shrine Museum near Shizuoka, is traditionally associated with Ieyasu's early career. It is a beautifully designed 'battledress' armour with a *zunari kabuto* style of helmet with smooth reflecting surfaces. Ieyasu is galloping along with his sword drawn. Beside him are Jodo monks bearing a white banner on which is written, 'Renounce this filthy world and attain the Pure Land', a flag that he would have with him in all future conflicts. Their Ikko-ikki opponents, who are simply dressed but heavily armed, counter with different Buddhist slogans on their war banners: 'Hail Amida Buddha' and the more ominous, 'He who advances is sure of heaven, but he who retreats is certain of damnation'. When the impetuous young Ieyasu retired to Okazaki Castle after this battle two spent bullets fell out of his shirt.

Warrior monks from the Jodo sect to which Ieyasu inclined are shown here in this lively print fighting for him against the Ikko-ikki army of the True Pure Land sect during the series of campaigns fought in Mikawa Province.

assist him in regaining Suruga. Ujizane had little scope for negotiation, so Ieyasu acquired Totomi and then quickly abandoned the Takeda alliance. Such manipulation of allies was common in the Sengoku Period, and the rewards for Ieyasu were great because the number of his followers grew when he acquired the samurai that lived in Totomi, including the famous Ii family.

In 1569 Ieyasu received imperial permission to resume the surname of Tokugawa, the name of the lineage that linked the Matsudaira to the Minamoto. This was a very significant development because it opened the way for Ieyasu to become shogun when all his ambitions were realized. He began by reorganizing his territory. In 1570 he moved his capital to Hamamatsu in Totomi, leaving Okazaki in the charge of his son Nobuyasu. That same year he joined Nobunaga for an expedition against the Asai and Asakura families, which was eventually to result in the battle of Anegawa. Here the Tokugawa troops gave a good account of themselves on Nobunaga's behalf, earning both glory and admiration.

Mikatagahara – the successful defeat

Two years later Tokugawa Ieyasu fought the battle that he would probably have most liked to forget. At the battle of Mikatagahara, which took place at a very short distance from his own castle of Hamamatsu, all of Ieyasu's achievements very nearly evaporated. It provides an example of Ieyasu at his best as a commander and also at his worst, so we will study it in some detail.

When Ieyasu moved his headquarters from Okazaki to Hamamatsu in 1570 the Takeda regarded it as a highly provocative act, because Hamamatsu lies almost at the mouth of the Tenryugawa, the river that drained the mountains of Takeda Shingen's territory. The result was a mighty showdown between the old power of the Takeda and the up-and-coming young daimyo. The backbone of Takeda Shingen's army was still his renowned mounted samurai. His old enemy Uesugi Kenshin was less of a threat to him

In this section from a modern painted screen at the Oichi Memorial Hall in Nagahama we see Tokugawa Ieyasu's troops advancing to the attack during the battle of Anegawa in 1570.

now that they had fought their fifth and final battle at Kawanakajima in 1564. Although powerful, the moment was not yet opportune for Shingen to enter the national stage because he still had no easy access to the Tokaido Road. The Tokugawa possessions would give him this, so Tokugawa Ieyasu's new base at Hamamatsu became Shingen's first objective. Takeda Shingen had also reached a new understanding with Hojo Ujimasa on his eastern flank, who had become his son-in-law. One result of the new Takeda/Hojo alliance was that Imagawa Ujizane, the son of the late Imagawa Yoshimoto, was banished from the Hojo domain, and went to seek refuge with the man who had once abandoned him – Tokugawa Ieyasu. Such was the nature of alliance building in Sengoku Japan!

When the threat to Hamamatsu became apparent Nobunaga advised Ieyasu to withdraw to Okazaki and avoid any conflict with Shingen. But Ieyasu would have none of it. He was now 29 years old, an experienced leader of samurai and a very determined young man. Retreat, any retreat, was beneath his samurai dignity, so Tokugawa Ieyasu stayed defiantly in Hamamatsu Castle as Takeda Shingen marched his army out of Tsutsujigasaki (modern Kofu) in October 1572. Shingen's first objective in the Tokugawa lands was the castle of Futamata. Its capture was entrusted to his son and heir Takeda Katsuyori, who is unfortunately known to history because of his defeat at Nagashino in 1575, but at Futamata he displayed his military talents with some style. Katsuyori had observed that the garrison of Futamata, which was built on the edge of a cliff over the Tenryugawa, collected their water supply from the river by lowering buckets from a rather elaborate wooden water tower. Katsuyori conceived the clever idea of floating heavy wooden rafts down the river to strike against the water tower's supports. The tower eventually collapsed and the garrison surrendered.

With Futamata lost Ieyasu was in extreme peril, but he had been joined in Hamamatsu by reinforcements sent by Nobunaga, all of whom were in favour

This statue of Tokugawa Ieyasu stands outside Hamamatsu Castle, the fortress in Totomi Province to which Ieyasu moved in 1570.

of not attacking Shingen. They reasoned that Shingen's objective was not Ieyasu, but Nobunaga himself, and that Hamamatsu should prepare for a siege. If Shingen's army moved on, leaving a masking force, then perhaps the siege could be broken and Shingen taken in the rear. It all made perfect sense, but Ieyasu was determined to stop Shingen by battle rather than a siege, and it had been reported to him that the Takeda army was drawn up in full battle order on the high ground of Mikatagahara just to the north of Hamamatsu Castle. The sight of such a host at close hand encouraged Ieyasu's commanders to persuade him again to hold back and let the Takeda march past into Mikawa so that they could conveniently fall upon their rear at a later stage. Once again Ieyasu turned down the suggestion, and decided to give battle.

The Tokugawa army marched out of the security of Hamamatsu at about four o'clock in the afternoon as the snow was beginning to fall. Aware of their approach, Takeda Shingen took up a strong defensive position from which the advancing Tokugawa could be enveloped. The first shots came when the front ranks of the Tokugawa opened fire on the Takeda samurai. The Takeda forward troops then attacked with great vigour. Ieyasu's men withstood the assault well, but the three commanders sent as reinforcements by Nobunaga did not have the same spirit for a desperate fight, particularly when they believed that Ieyasu's decision had been wrong.

At this point the power of the renowned Takeda cavalry came into its own. They were not charging a defensive line as they would do at Nagashino three years later. Instead they were advancing against disordered troops. It was the situation for which the 'demon horsemen of Kai', as they were known, had been waiting, and they were led forward across the frozen ground by Takeda Katsuyori, who proved himself to be a fine leader of horsemen. It was now getting dark, and seeing the Tokugawa troops reeling Shingen ordered a general assault by the main body. The charge by the mounted Takeda samurai had proved its worth, and very soon the Tokugawa army was in full retreat. Ieyasu sent Okubo Tadayo back to plant Ieyasu's personal golden fan standard as a rallying point for the troops. Ieyasu himself was still in a fighting mood, and was all for charging back into the Takeda ranks to assist his comrade Mizuno Masashige, who was surrounded, or to die in the attempt. By now the Takeda had reached Ieyasu's headquarters troops and were surrounding his bodyguard, when Natsume Yoshinobu, the commander of Hamamatsu

Opposite:
1. Takeda Shingen leaves Tsutsujigasaki to attack Hamamatsu.
2. Shingen captures Futamata.
3. Shingen advances to Mikatagahara where Ieyasu joins him in battle.
4. Shingen returns on campaign in 1573 but dies at Noda.
5. Takeda Katsuyori is defeated by Oda Nobunaga and Tokugawa Ieyasu at Nagashino in 1575.
6. Route of Ieyasu and Oda Nobutada's two-pronged advance into Kai in 1582.
7. Takeda Katsuyori is defeated at Temmokuzan in 1582.

Ieyasu's campaigns against the Takeda, 1570–82

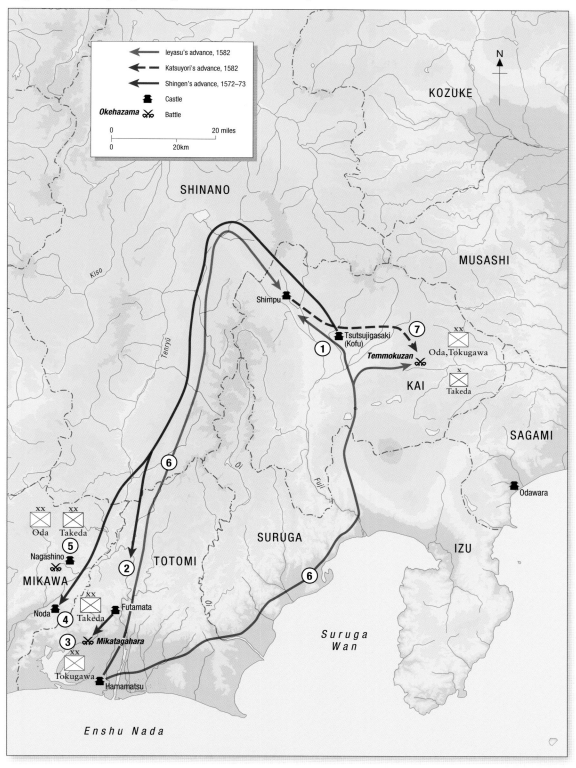

Legend:
- Ieyasu's advance, 1582
- Katsuyori's advance, 1582
- Shingen's advance, 1572–73
- Castle
- *Okehazama* Battle
- 0 — 20 miles
- 0 — 20km

KOZUKE

SHINANO

MUSASHI

Kiso

Shimpu

Tenryū

Tsutsujigasaki
(Kofu)

①

Temmokuzan

⑦

xx
Oda, Tokugawa

KAI

x
Takeda

SAGAMI

Ōi

⑥

Fuji

IZU

Odawara

xx   xx
Oda   Takeda

⑤

Nagashino

MIKAWA

SURUGA

②

TOTOMI

⑥

Noda

xx
Takeda

Futamata

④

③ *Mikatagahara*

xx
Tokugawa

Hamamatsu

Suruga Wan

Enshu Nada

19

Following the battle of Mikatagahara the Tokugawa forces retreated to Hamamatsu Castle, where Sakai Tadatsugu beat the war drum in the gate tower to raise morale.

Castle, rode out from the fortress to persuade his lord to withdraw, and to hold back the enemy while he did so. But Ieyasu was in no mood to listen, so with the authority granted to him solely by his age, Yoshinobu tugged on Ieyasu's bridle to bring his horse around, and struck it on the rump with his spear shaft, calling out to Ieyasu's attendants to ride with their lord for the castle. Hoping to mislead the Takeda, Yoshinobu turned back to the Takeda shouting 'I am Ieyasu!' and plunged into the fight to be killed. Amano Yasukage, who survived the action, kicked the bow out of a Takeda soldier's hands as he took aim at Ieyasu, so the withdrawal must have been a closely fought action. Ieyasu himself put an arrow through one Takeda man who ran at him with a spear.

To put heart into the defenders of Hamamatsu Castle, Ieyasu had earlier sent to the castle a samurai who had cut the head from a warrior wearing a monk's cowl, which he claimed to be the head of Takeda Shingen, but the brief deception had given them only a temporary respite from worry, and the rapid arrival of Ieyasu with apparently only five men left made it appear that defeat was certain. Torii Mototada was just giving orders for the gates to be shut and barred when Ieyasu interrupted him. To shut the gates was precisely what Takeda Shingen expected them to do, he reasoned. Instead he ordered for the gates to be left open for their retreating comrades, and huge braziers to be lit to guide them home. To add

Tokugawa Ieyasu leads his army out of Hamamatsu Castle to the battlefield of Mikatagahara

By 1572 Ieyasu now owned the adjacent Totomi Province in addition to Mikawa. He made Hamamatsu in Totomi his new capital, a move that enraged Takeda Shingen, who advanced out of Kai and captured the strategic Futamata Castle. The Takeda army was stationed on the plain of Mikatagahara a few miles to the north. Rather than face a siege, Ieyasu decided to march out of Hamamatsu and give battle, a move contrary to the advice of all his allies and supporters.

In this plate we see Ieyasu (1) as determined as he was at Azukizaka, and as events were to show, almost as reckless over his personal safety. For now, as he leaves the gates of Hamamatsu on a dull winter afternoon when the first flakes of snow are falling, he looks more like an experienced general marching towards his fate. The full heraldry of the future shogun is now on display, including his vivid golden sun standard (2), the Jodo banner (3) and the other flags born by men who are both strong and brave. Again we do not know for certain which armour Ieyasu wore on this occasion, but the modern statue of him outside the gate of Hamamatsu shows him in this striking design with his favourite helmet bearing a golden fern *maedate* (crest) (4). This armour is also preserved at the Kunozan Toshogu.

to the confident air, Sakai Tadatsugu took a large war drum and beat it in the tower beside the gate. His lord, apparently well satisfied with the precautions they had taken, took a meal of three bowls of rice and went to sleep. As Ieyasu had predicted, when the Takeda advanced to the castle and saw the open gates and the light and heard the drum, they immediately suspected a trick. They also noted that the Tokugawa dead who had all died in the advance lay face downwards, while those killed in the retreat lay on their backs. None had turned their backs to the enemy. The Tokugawa samurai were men to be reckoned with, so no night-time assault was made on the castle, and what 'siege lines' there may have been were just the bivouacs of the Takeda army who camped for the night on the battlefield near Saigadake. The weather conditions indicated that it would be an uncomfortable stay, so the Tokugawa men resolved to make it as unpleasant as possible, thereby keeping up the fiction of a strongly defended castle. It was an area the Tokugawa men knew well, so they gathered a volunteer force of 16 musketeers and 100 other footsoldiers and attacked the Takeda encampment at Saigadake, where a narrow canyon splits the plain of Mikatagahara. The Tokugawa troops led the Takeda back to this ravine, which is about 30m deep in places. Many scores of Takeda samurai and horses fell into this ravine, where the Tokugawa troops fired on them and cut them down as they lay helpless. After the battle,

This is the actual war drum from Hamamatsu Castle used during the battle of Mikatagahara. It is kept in Iwata, the town next to Hamamatsu.

according to legend, local people were troubled by the moans from the ghosts coming from this valley, so in 1574 Ieyasu established a temple at Saigadake called the Soen-do, where a monk called Soen prayed for the repose of the souls. In recent years, when the stream that runs through Saigadake was being culverted, bodies were found under the surface of the ground.

All the signs now pointed towards a long and desperate siege, and the snows were just beginning. If only the Takeda had known the truth about how weakly Hamamatsu was actually defended they could have taken it by assault, but in the event Takeda Shingen held a council of war and resolved to withdraw to his mountains and return the following year, rather than risk a winter siege of Hamamatsu. So the whole Takeda army pulled back, fooled completely by the Tokugawa resolve.

Ieyasu had had a narrow escape at Mikatagahara. Takeda Shingen returned to attack Totomi the following year only to die while besieging Ieyasu's Noda Castle. It was a fortuitous development, and Ieyasu was soon to share in Nobunaga's great victory of Nagashino over Takeda Shingen's heir Katsuyori in 1575. This famous battle was not immediately decisive, and for the next few years Ieyasu patiently pursued the Takeda into their mountains, until, with the help of Nobutada, Oda Nobunaga's son, Takeda Katsuyori was defeated at the battle of Temmokuzan in 1582. Ieyasu received the former Takeda provinces of Kai and Shinano as a reward from Nobunaga. He then consolidated his position, allowing Hideyoshi to succeed Nobunaga when the latter was murdered in 1582. This was always one of Ieyasu's great skills: that of knowing when not to get involved in developments.

The Komaki–Nagakute campaign

By 1584 Ieyasu was lord of five provinces (Mikawa, Totomi, Suruga, Kai and Shinano) and his sphere of influence collided with Hideyoshi's during the Komaki–Nagakute campaign of 1584, so called from the two engagements that took place. The campaign provides an excellent example of thoughtful strategy on the part of both commanders followed by furious battling, and an occasion when the divisions into which an army was split had great bearing on the outcome of a battle. We see armies spread out so much that rearguards are assaulted by vanguards,

who are then surprised themselves in spite of the vigilance of scouts.

The epic campaign began when Hideyoshi's ally Ikeda Nobuteru took the castle of Inuyama, on the Kiso River. Ieyasu had established his forward base at Nobunaga's former castle of Kiyosu. The capture of Inuyama was thus an indirect move against Ieyasu, and when Ikeda's son-in-law Mori Nagayoshi was seen to be moving along the road from Inuyama towards Kiyosu, Ieyasu decided to stop the advance while the force was still isolated. Sakai Tadatsugu and others took a detachment of the Tokugawa force, 5,000 strong, and met the Mori army halfway along the road at Komaki. Here a fierce battle ensued. Mori managed to hold the Tokugawa force in the village in spite of heavy harquebus fire, until Sakai circled round and attacked him from the rear. Mori hastily retreated with the loss of 300 men. Sakakibara Yasumasa then suggested that Ieyasu should move his headquarters up to Komaki, for near the village was a ruined castle on a rounded hill 200m high that dominated the flat rice lands. So the Tokugawa force dug trenches and erected palisades around Komakiyama. The building of fortifications took a week, and, as no immediate danger threatened, Ieyasu ordered the repair of two old castles at Hira and Kobata.

We are also told that Ieyasu built a military road to connect Komaki with a series of forts out to the south-east. This was almost certainly fortified, at least as far as Hachimanzuka, a conclusion drawn from Hideyoshi's response to it. On 7 May Hideyoshi had entered Inuyama Castle, where Ikeda Nobuteru apprised him of developments. A reconnaissance of Ieyasu's position at Komaki showed that both of Hideyoshi's own two front-line forts of Iwasakiyama and Futaebori were on ground lower than Komaki. Hideyoshi therefore ordered the construction of a long rampart to join the two together

On the night following the retreat from Mikatagahara Ieyasu arranged an ambush for the pursuing Takeda samurai at Saigadake, where a river gorge split the plain. This picture of modern Saigadake indicates very well the depth of the narrow river valley.

via the fort of Tanaka. The resulting earthwork, probably strengthened with wood, was completed overnight. It was over 2km long, 3m high and 2m thick, and was pierced with several gates to allow a counterattack. The slope of the rampart also allowed for the provision of firing positions. Satisfied with his defensive front line, Hideyoshi set up his headquarters to the rear at Gakuden, which was linked to Tanaka by a series of communications forts.

From behind their lines both commanders waited, fearing to launch a frontal attack and meet the fate of Takeda Katsuyori at Nagashino. Hideyoshi had no fewer than 80,000 men under his command, and was rather bored by the situation, because he wrote to a colleague that as Ieyasu would not come out and fight him they might as well go home. It was obvious that such a stalemate could not last long in Sengoku Japan, and after less than a week of waiting, Ikeda Nobuteru went to Hideyoshi and suggested a raid on Mikawa Province. As half the samurai from Mikawa were now sitting behind palisades on Komakiyama this sounded a reasonable suggestion if surprise could be guaranteed. Hideyoshi agreed, and prepared to launch a frontal attack on Ieyasu's positions as a diversion.

Ikeda set off on his raid at midnight, 15/16 May. His force numbered 20,000, and, as an aid to secrecy with such a large host, Ikeda divided his forces for the march. It was a risky strategy, but for the first two days at least communications seem to have been maintained within his army. Ikeda Nobuteru left first with 6,000 men, followed by Mori Nagayoshi with 3,000, Hori Hidemasa with 3,000 and Miyoshi Hidetsugu with 8,000. The dawn of 16 May found them camping beside a forest called Hakuzan. An army of 20,000 is not easy to conceal, and that afternoon some farmers informed Ieyasu of the presence of a large number of enemy samurai. At first he was disinclined to believe them, but that evening a scout confirmed the report, and Ieyasu prepared to move. By this time, of course, Ikeda's army had moved on, more slowly now, marching through the day after a short rest. On the night of 16/17 May the raiding army was heading for Iwasaki, a fort held for Ieyasu by Niwa Ujishige. The army was now spread over about 8km, and at

A head and shoulders portrait of Tokugawa Ieyasu in the Nagashino Castle Preservation Hall. Ieyasu's participation in the famous battle of Nagashino further endeared him to Oda Nobunaga. Over the next seven years Ieyasu joined Nobunaga's son Nobutada in a long campaign that eventually destroyed the Takeda clan.

Opposite:
1. Ikeda Nobutero captures Inuyama.
2. Mori Nagayoshi advances towards Haguro.
3. Tokugawa Ieyasu moves up to Komaki, secures it and engages Mori at Haguro.
4. Ieyasu fortifies Komaki and links it to other forts.
5. Toyotomi Hideyoshi moves to Gakuden via Haguro and establishes a fortified line between Iwasakiyama and Futaebori.
6. Ikeda Nobutero leaves the line for a surprise raid on Mikawa.
7. He rests at Hakuzan only to have his rearguard attacked.
8. The vanguard of Ikeda's army attack Iwasaki.
9. Hori Hidemasa wheels his army round to face the Tokugawa advance.
10. The armies clash at Nagakute.

The showdown with Hideyoshi: the Komaki–Nagakute campaign, 1584

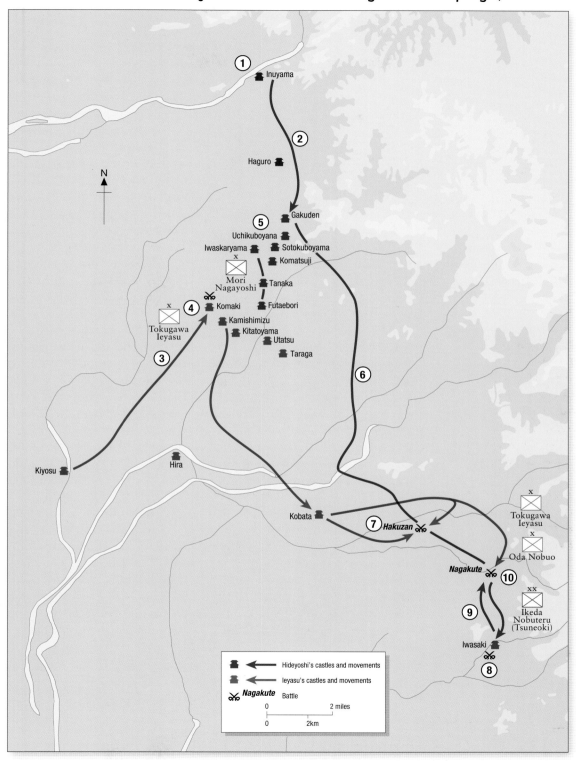

Legend:

🏯 ← Hideyoshi's castles and movements
🏯 ← Ieyasu's castles and movements
⚔ *Nagakute* Battle

0 — 2 miles
0 — 2km

Iwasaki Castle was the objective of Hideyoshi's raid into Mikawa Province that caught Ieyasu off guard in his fortified line at Komaki. This operation led to the battle of Nagakute.

dawn on 17 May Ikeda's vanguard assaulted Iwasaki, which they took with little trouble.

Ikeda's success, however, had been achieved only by his vanguard. The rest of the army were still nowhere in sight, and were in fact eating their breakfast at Hakuzan, oblivious of the victory and also ignorant of the fact that the Tokugawa army was in pursuit of them. Ieyasu had in fact left his lines at 8pm on the evening of 16 May. His advance guard under Mizuno Tadashige had reached Kobata about 10pm, where they were joined by Ieyasu at midnight. Ieyasu had correctly guessed Ikeda's strategy and had also worked out that his army would be strung out along the road and therefore very vulnerable.

Ieyasu's general Mizuno Tadashige was allowed a two-hour sleep and was then sent to catch the rearguard of Ikeda's army. The surprise was complete. The Ikeda rearguard under Miyoshi Hidetsugu was suddenly attacked by Mizuno Tadashige from the right and Sakakibara Yasubara from the left. The attack was completely successful, and Miyoshi only just managed to escape with his head. His third division, who were the nearest source of help, lay about 3 miles farther along the road, but the sound of harquebus fire reached them before the mounted courier guards. Realizing that something serious was happening Hori Hidemasa quickly wheeled his army round and marched back towards the sound of firing. They soon reached the village of Nagakute, and, seeing that the Tokugawa troops were still advancing, he took up positions in two companies on a hill, with a small river between them and the advancing enemy.

It was 7 on the morning of 17 May. Hori ordered his men to light their matches, and load so that they were ready to fire when the enemy were about 15m away. As an added inducement he offered 100 koku of rice to anyone who brought down a horseman. On came the Tokugawa troops at a run, straight into the range of the harquebuses. A hail of bullets swept their ranks, and seeing them reel Hori led his men in a vigorous charge which flung the Tokugawa samurai aside. But as Hori's 3,000 hit the Tokugawa 4,500 and split them wide open, Hori saw on the horizon the golden fan standard of Ieyasu leading the Tokugawa main body. Once again the surpriser had been surprised. Hori prudently withdrew, and again took up his position together with the first and second divisions under Mori and Ikeda, who had hurried back from Iwasaki to join him. Tokugawa Ieyasu made a wide sweep as he arrived, collecting up the remnants of his vanguard.

There was a pause while both armies dressed their ranks, and then at 9am the second phase of the battle of Nagakute began with the Tokugawa harquebusiers blazing away at their opponents. This goaded the two Ikeda sons into attacking Ii Naomasa, who held them off with fierce harquebus fire. Ikeda senior moved over to aid his sons, but neither Mori nor Ieyasu had yet fired a shot. Mori was waiting for Ieyasu to support his left wing, whereupon Mori could take him in flank, but Ieyasu was not fooled. He suddenly charged his whole contingent forward in two sections, and the impact alone made Mori's samurai stagger. Mori rode up and down in front of his lines and waved his war fan frantically. He stood out conspicuously in his white surcoat, and one of the Ii ashigaru took careful aim and shot him through the head. It was a very public death, and acted as a signal for Oda Nobuo to swoop round and fall on Mori's flank. In vain did Ikeda Nobuteru send his men forward in support. The whole Mori force gave way, and Ikeda collapsed on his camp stool knowing that all was lost. A young samurai ran up and speared him through, acquiring a prize head. By 1pm the battle was over. Ieyasu sat down and was shown 2,500 heads of the defeated. He was pleased to hear that their own losses had been fewer than 600.

Meanwhile, back at the two bases, speculation was growing about the outcome of the expedition. When Hideyoshi heard of the early morning encounter he immediately set off with reinforcements, while Honda Tadakatsu made ready to take him in flank. In fact, it never came to a battle, for Hideyoshi's force was so vast as to make him extremely sympathetic to Honda's bravery, and although they could have annihilated the talented Tokugawa captain they did not even threaten him. Honda therefore carried on to Kobata, where he met Ieyasu for a parley. Soon both armies were safe behind their lines, and the previous stalemate began again. In fact no frontal attack between the two ever took place at Komaki, and the ramparts were eventually allowed to crumble back into the rice fields. Just as the ramparts crumbled, so did the enmity between Hideyoshi and Ieyasu, and the military lives of both were to be kept separate for many years.

THE HOUR OF DESTINY

From 1584 onwards, a time when Hideyoshi firmly established himself as the greatest power in Japan, Ieyasu showed that discretion was part of his political and military genius by being highly selective about which of Hideyoshi's campaigns he wished to participate in, and six years after Komaki–Nagakute he undertook an expedition on Hideyoshi's behalf that involved him in little effort but gained him an immense reward. Having avoided service in the invasions of Shikoku (1585) and Kyushu (1587), Ieyasu could hardly refuse to be involved in the siege of the Hojo's Odawara Castle in 1590, because the Hojo's domain of the Kanto plain was immediately adjacent to his own. The Tokugawa troops were among the few to see real action at Odawara, and when the Hojo capitulated Hideyoshi struck a deal with Ieyasu whereby he would surrender his existing provinces in return for the Hojo's former territories.

Ieyasu agreed, and took over the eight provinces of the Kanto, although he did not make Odawara his capital. Instead he established it at Edo, a modest-sized fishing village with an accompanying castle. Little Edo is now the city of Tokyo.

In 1592, by pleading the difficulty of the vast distance his domains lay from the assembly point in Kyushu, Ieyasu also avoided service in the bloodbath of Korea. This left his own army in better shape than those of the daimyo who suffered in that ill-fated campaign. These were the men who were soon to take sides between Toyotomi Hideyori, the infant heir of Hideyoshi, and Tokugawa Ieyasu, who was rapidly approaching his hour of destiny.

A reproduction of the gold *maedate* (helmet frontlet) in the shape of a fern that was worn by Ieyasu on one of his favourite helmets. It is on show in the Sekigahara Museum.

The Sekigahara War

Tokugawa Ieyasu's hour of destiny can be summed up in one word – Sekigahara, 'the moor of the barrier', a strategic valley in Mino Province (modern Gifu Prefecture) where two vital roads met and the place where, on a foggy October morning in 1600, Ieyasu fought one of the most decisive battles in Japanese history. Yet Sekigahara was more than just a battle. Events that occurred elsewhere in Japan could have prevented the great showdown from happening, or even nullified its results, and as these conflicts took place simultaneously in Kyushu, Central Japan and Tohoku, even the term 'the Sekigahara campaign' is insufficient to do justice to the situation. So many families were involved and so many battles fought that it was as if the whole century-long drama of the Sengoku Period was being replayed in two frantic months. Nor was the actual battle of Sekigahara immediately decisive. It was enough of a victory to allow Ieyasu to disarm or liquidate his opponents, to restore the shogunate and to set in motion a massive scheme of land transfer, but a potent focus of opposition still remained afterwards in the person of Toyotomi Hideyori, the child in whose name the great battle was fought. Hideyori never left the security of Osaka Castle during the whole of the 1600 campaign, and it would be 1615 before he and his stubborn supporters were finally destroyed and the hegemony established by Ieyasu made safe. For all these reasons I shall use the expression 'The Sekigahara War' for the complex series of events that made up Ieyasu's hour of destiny in 1600, and shall then conclude it with the dramatic epilogue

Opposite:
1. 28 August: Ieyasu arrives in Edo from the West.
2. 2 September: council of war is held at Oyama.
3. 30 September: fall of Gifu.
4. 1 October: Eastern Army arrives at Akasaka and set up a position.
5. 7 October: Ieyasu leaves Edo.
6. 11 October: Hidetada begins siege of Ueda.
7. 13 October: siege of Otsu begins.
8. 20 October: battle of Kuisegawa.
9. 21 October: battle of Sekigahara.
10. 23 October: fall of Ogaki and Sawayama.
11. 2 November: Ieyasu enters Osaka.

The Sekigahara War, 1600

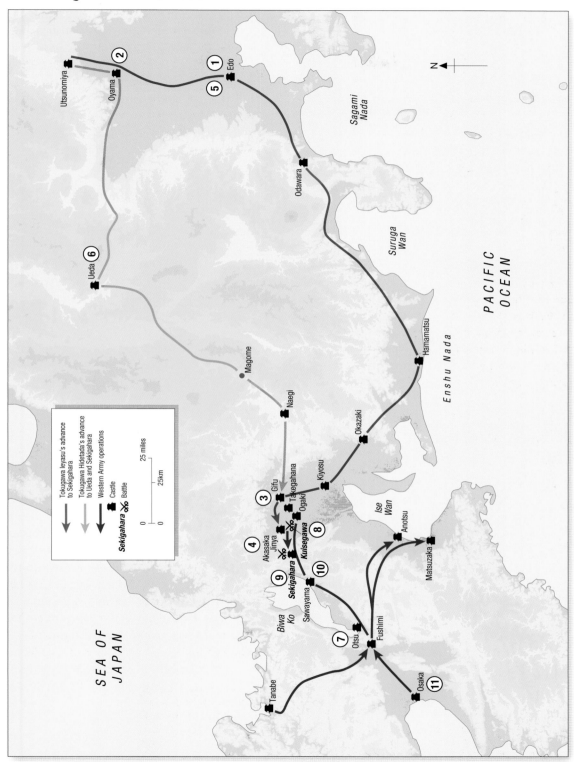

This magnificent painted scroll at Okazaki depicts Tokugawa Ieyasu as a general. He is wearing a fine *yoroi* armour and sits on a raised dais, sword in hand.

at Osaka in 1615 that proved to be its consolidation.

If Sekigahara is accepted as being a war rather than just a battle the conclusions that we are able to draw regarding Ieyasu's abilities as a commander become very far-reaching, because he was absolutely in charge of the whole operation. As commander-in-chief of the 'Eastern Army' (who fought Ishida Mitsunari's 'Western Army'), Ieyasu was intimately involved with every aspect of the political movements and strategic planning that set each scenario in motion. Ieyasu then relied on and trusted his generals in the field to achieve their individual objectives, and in only one instance, that of his own son and heir, did this policy disappoint. We therefore see an excellent example of warfare by delegation. At the battle of Sekigahara itself Ieyasu took personal command and assumed full responsibility for the tactical decisions on the day. Fourteen years later he was to repeat the process at Osaka on a smaller political and strategic scale, though a greater tactical scale, to consolidate his achievement. The Sekigahara War, therefore, was more than Ieyasu's hour of destiny: it was the time when all his skills came to the fore and all his old weaknesses were overcome to present him as a truly great commander.

The phoney war

When Toyotomi Hideyoshi was approaching death in 1598 his greatest concern was to safeguard the inheritance of his infant son Hideyori, in whom he had invested all his hopes. Hideyori had been born in 1593, and so optimistic was Hideyoshi for his succession that he had disinherited his previously named heir: his adopted son Hidetsugu, who was forced to commit suicide following spurious accusations of treason. There was now no one other than this five-year-old child to inherit the newly reunified Japan, so to protect Hideyori's interests Hideyoshi appointed a board of five regents from the ranks of his most loyal vassals. The men chosen were Tokugawa Ieyasu, Maeda Toshiie, the daimyo of Kaga who had not long to live, Ukita Hideie, the former commander-in-chief of the Korean expedition, Mori Terumoto who dominated western Honshu (the main island of Japan) and Uesugi Kagekatsu who was based in Tohoku. They were to rule above the heads of the existing five *bugyo* ('magistrates' or 'commissioners'): Masuda Nagamori, Ishida Mitsunari, Maeda Munehisa, Asano Nagamasa and Nagatsuka Masaie. Hideyoshi also thought it prudent to give three other daimyo a role as go-betweens. These were Ikoma Chikamasa, Nakamura Kazuuji and Horio Yoshiharu. It sounded a good idea but was a recipe for disaster. Japan was now to be ruled by a committee whose domains were spread widely across the country and whose personal feelings for each other were not always of an affectionate kind. Ieyasu saw their weaknesses, realized his own strength and almost immediately went to war with his colleagues.

At first the Sekigahara War was a phoney war, with Ieyasu deliberately causing political divisions and provoking reactions to establish where each of them lay. He began by arranging four political marriages for his family, a practice that Hideyoshi had strictly forbidden because of the

dissension it caused, to strengthen his relationships with the powerful daimyo Date Masamune, Fukushima Masanori, Hachisuka Yoshishige and Konishi Yukinaga. There was some opposition to the move, particularly from the *bugyo* Ishida Mitsunari, but the absence of a unified condemnation of Ieyasu provided valuable intelligence about potential divisions, and gradually such lines became more clearly drawn with Ishida Mitsunari becoming identified as the main leader of opposition to his rise to power. In such a climate assassination would not have been out of place as a means to an end, and indeed may have been considered on both sides. Ieyasu certainly held back from such a move against Ishida Mitsunari, because even though he was far from being the most powerful of the daimyo who were likely to oppose a Tokugawa takeover, Ieyasu felt that Ishida had the personality most likely to bring opposition to a head, so that for the time being at any rate he was of more use alive than dead.

Ieyasu was currently residing in Fushimi Castle to the south-east of Kyoto, a mighty fortress built by Hideyoshi to defend the capital. It was not far away from Osaka where Toyotomi Hideyori lived, and to demonstrate that he had no evil intentions towards the child Ieyasu stayed in Osaka Castle

In this small area of the 'bloody ceiling' of the Yogen-In Temple in Kyoto we see an unmistakeable hand-print left by one of the samurai who committed suicide with Torii Mototada at the siege of Fushimi Castle in 1600.

Chiyo was the wife of Yamanouchi Kazutoyo and sent a secret message to her husband advising him to join Ieyasu's party. The message was twisted into the cord of the messenger's helmet.

with him for the first few months of 1600, thus filling the gap left by his personal guardian Maeda Toshiie, who had died in 1599. It was a gesture of self-confidence that was not wasted on the others, who were beginning to realize that Ieyasu wanted to seize power. But Ieyasu had always to keep a keen eye on the developments in the north-east of Japan. His domains in the Kanto lay at a considerable distance from the capital, and Uesugi Kagekatsu had the potential to threaten Tokugawa

The Sanada family posed a major threat to Tokugawa Ieyasu along the length of the Nakasendo Road. But they were a house divided. Here we see a waxworks in Ueda Castle that shows Sanada Masayuki with his two sons in 1586, making the decision to send his elder son Nobuyuki as a hostage to the Tokugawa. Nobuyuki married into the Tokugawa retainer band and became a loyal Tokugawa supporter.

interests from Tohoku. Therein lay Ieyasu's greatest dilemma – different threats at vastly separate distances – so when intelligence was brought to him that Uesugi Kagekatsu was building a new castle to replace his existing capital at Wakamatsu (modern Aizu-Wakamatsu, Fukushima Prefecture) he sent messages requesting Kagekatsu to visit Kyoto and explain his actions. Kagekatsu consistently refused to do this, hoping that Ieyasu would be forced to vacate his position of power around Kyoto and Osaka and head east. This, to put it crudely, was Uesugi's game, so that once Ieyasu was separated both from Hideyori and his supporters in central Japan, the anti-Tokugawa party could establish a firm base in the west while Uesugi destroyed him in the east.

Tokugawa Ieyasu saw through all their scheming, so that when he eventually set off from Fushimi Castle on 28 July, ostensibly to face the threat from Uesugi, he took the journey very slowly, keeping in touch with developments at his rear and prepared always to march back if necessary. In fact Uesugi Kagekatsu worried him much less than his opponents believed because of secret alliances Ieyasu had made with the other lords of Tohoku, particularly Date Masamune and Mogami Yoshiaki. The real threat, Ieyasu understood correctly, lay in the west. He arrived in Edo a full month later on 28 August, and then established himself at Oyama in Shimotsuke Province (modern Tochigi Prefecture) on 1 September, from where his son Hidetada was taking charge of the operation against Uesugi. There, on the following day a council of war was held, and it may have been at that meeting that the news arrived that Ishida Mitsunari had taken advantage of Ieyasu's departure and was advancing against Fushimi Castle. The phoney war was over and the real one had begun.

The fight for castles

The over-riding conclusion drawn by Ieyasu's council of war, which was attended by Fukushima Masanari, Kuroda Nagamasa, Hosokawa Tadaoki, Ikeda Terumasa, Kato Yoshiaki and Asano Yoshinaga, was that the west was indeed the main theatre of operations and that the threat from Uesugi Kagekatsu could be contained by Ieyasu's supporters in Tohoku, leaving the rest of the Tokugawa allies free to head back west. In fact moves against Uesugi Kagekatsu, which history was to dub the Tohoku Sekigahara campaign, had already begun with an assault on Shiroishi Castle to the south of Sendai on the same day that Ieyasu arrived at Oyama. It took one day to fall, and then Date Masamune could safely move west over the central mountains of Tohoku to take the fight directly to Uesugi.

Yet the prize of Shiroishi Castle was to be overbalanced by the immeasurably greater loss of Fushimi. This occurred on 8 September, after one of the greatest castle-based actions in Japanese history. Fushimi's strategic importance had been well appreciated by Hideyoshi when he built this multi-baileyed fortress, which now lay under the command of Torii Mototada, once Ieyasu's childhood playmate and now the man to whom Ieyasu would delegate responsibility for the single most important Tokugawa possession west of Edo. Torii Mototada rose to the occasion, and held off a series of furious attacks (there was no time for a long conventional siege) by Ukita Hideie and others over a period of ten days. Eventually a man whose wife and children had been seized by the besiegers set one of the towers in the outer defences on fire from within. In this way a breach was made in the outer defences, but still Torii would not surrender. He reasoned that as Ieyasu would be marching westwards to engage Ishida and his allies in battle, the longer he could delay the inevitable end the better for the Tokugawa

cause. So the war of attrition at Fushimi continued until the inner courtyard was full of enemy soldiers and Torii Mototada was down to a handful of followers. Exhausted, Mototada sat down on a step and was recognized by a samurai who graciously allowed him to commit suicide. His head was then taken. One account of the end at Fushimi has the castle burning like a gigantic funeral pyre, but this is contradicted in part at least by the existence in Kyoto of three temples with 'bloody ceilings' made from the blood-stained floorboards where Torii and his companions cut themselves open. The most dramatic of all, in the Yogen-In next to the Sanjusangendo Temple, bears an unmistakable bloody hand-print.

Fushimi was lost, but other castles could still be won and would have to be won if Ieyasu was to secure his communications along the two main

Komatsu-dono was the wife of Sanada Nobuyuki and played a vital role in her husband's efforts on behalf of Tokugawa Ieyasu by her defence of the castle of Numata.

Ueda Castle was the biggest obstacle to Tokugawa Hidetada's progress along the Nakasendo Road. His siege of it, which may have been unnecessary, meant that he missed the great battle of Sekigahara.

roads leading from Edo to Osaka. The first of these roads, the famous Tokaido, passed through both ancient and modern Tokugawa territory for much of its length. The other, the Nakasendo, which threaded its way through the mountains, was more hostile, so Ieyasu's strategy was as follows. First, an advance unit would use the Tokaido to secure castles on the approach to Kyoto and Ieyasu would follow along this route later. Second, his son Tokugawa Hidetada would

Naegi, near Nakatsugawa in Gifu Prefecture, is one of Japan's oddest castle sites. Because of the rounded rocks on its summit the keep was built on top of a huge wooden framework locked into grooves cut in the stone. Naegi had the potential to stop Tokugawa Hidetada's advance to Sekigahara had it not been for a quick raid by Toyama Tomomasa who captured it.

undertake the difficult journey along the Nakasendo, securing or otherwise neutralizing enemy fortresses along the way.

The first division that left Oyama and Edo along the Tokaido consisted of 16,000 men. It was led by Fukushima Masanori and included Hosokawa Tadaoki, Kato Yoshiaki, Kuroda Nagamasa, Todo Takatora, Honda Tadakatsu and Ii Naomasa. The second division was of 18,000 men under Ikeda Terumasa along with Asano Yukinaga (son of the *bugyo* Nagamasa), Yamanouchi Kazutoyo, Horio Yoshiharu and Arima Toyouji. The inclusion of names cited above as members of Hideyoshi's governing bodies gives an indication of how rapidly sides had been taken. In fact it had been a time of decision for everyone, although some on both sides had wavered. Yamanouchi Kazutoyo, for example, had been inclined to support Ishida and was preparing to march to join him when he received a secret message from his redoubtable and well-informed wife Chiyo urging him to side with Ieyasu. The message had been written on a piece of paper twisted into the helmet cord of the courier.

The first objective of the Tokugawa vanguard was to reinforce and secure possession of Kiyosu Castle. This place, for long associated with Oda Nobunaga, lay where the gap between the Tokaido and the Nakasendo was at its narrowest before they joined beside Lake Biwa. Fukushima Masanori owned it, and he had left it in the capable hands of a certain Osaki Gemba. Kiyosu was also uncomfortably close to Ogaki, to which Ishida Mitsunari had moved from his castle of Sawayama (near modern Hikone in Shiga Prefecture). Ogaki was to be Ishida's main position during the campaign, and from here he sent messages to Osaki Gemba to persuade him to surrender Kiyosu. Had Ishida carried out an assault as at Fushimi he may have succeeded in acquiring it. As it was, the rapid advance of Fukushima's division meant that Kiyosu was soon firmly reinforced.

The whole length of the Tokaido as far as Kiyosu had now been secured for Ieyasu's Eastern Army, but north of Kiyosu it was a very different story. Inaddition to Ueda high in the mountains of Shinano Province (modern Nagano Prefecture) the Western Army controlled a number of fortresses along the road or near to it as it approached Lake Biwa. These were Sawayama (Ishida's own castle near modern Hikone in Shiga Prefecture), Takegahana, Gifu (once Oda Nobunaga's mighty headquarters), Inuyama on a rock above the Kisogawa, and Ogaki, which lay just to the south of the Nakasendo.

The Eastern Army's sights were now firmly set on this group of fortresses. A council of war was held at Kiyosu, and the army of Fukushima Masanori launched an assault on Takegahana on 29 September. This was immediately successful, so he joined forces with Ikeda Terumasa for an attack on Gifu. The expression 'joined forces' may be a little idealistic in these circumstances, because Gifu was a major prize likely to yield both glory and reward, so both commanders were eager to embrace the traditional samurai obsession of being the first into battle. At first they advanced side by side but Ikeda's army was seen to be moving to the front, which provoked an angry response from Fukushima. Fortunately for Ieyasu the matter was settled amicably by Fukushima agreeing to attack the front gate while Ikeda attacked the rear. These were sensible tactics anyway because of Gifu's layout. What is nowadays called Gifu Castle is an isolated keep, originally little more than a lookout post on a very high mountain reached by cable car, with the key structures of the castle being down on the flatlands beside the river. This was what the friendly rivals attacked, and Gifu fell on 30 September. Its commander Oda Hidenobu fled for the sanctuary of the holy mountain of Koyasan.

While these operations were continuing the Western Army was taking steps to defend its friendly length of the Tokaido where it passed through Ise Province (modern Mie Prefecture). To the south of the road two castles lay in Eastern hands: Matsuzaka and Anotsu (modern Tsu). Matsuzaka, held by Furuta Shigekatsu, fell to an attack on 1 October, the day after Gifu had been lost. Meanwhile Mori Hidemoto (the cousin of Regent Terumoto) was attacking Anotsu, where four days of fighting ensued before the castle fell on 3 October, a long episode made more remarkable by the fact that a woman was defending Anotsu. This was Yuki no kata, the wife of the castle commander Tomita Nobutaka who was with Ieyasu.

The Eastern Army now assessed its gains and losses. They had lost Fushimi, Anotsu and Matsuzaka, but had secured much of the area where the two great roads were at their closest, leaving them able to threaten Ishida along the stretch between his home castle of Sawayama and his forward position of Ogaki. Thousands of Eastern troops were now in the area, so it was time for them to take up a position where they could await the arrival of their commander-in-chief Tokugawa Ieyasu and then move on to destroy Ishida Mitsunari on ground of their own choosing. The decision was

The castle of Ogaki, shown here in its restored state following its destruction in World War II, was the forward base for Ishida Mitsunari during the Sekigahara campaign. A fierce siege of Ogakai continued during the battle of Sekigahara. Ogaki, although built on a low hill, is an example of the *hirajiro* (castle on a plain) style.

The battle of Kuisegawa was a skirmish that acted as the curtain raiser for Sekigahara. Here we see the leader of the Western Army attack, Shima Sakon, in a painted screen at Sekigahara Warland.

made not to base the army in a castle but to erect a massive fortified camp at the village of Akasaka (modern Mino-Akasaka in Gifu Prefecture) that straddled the Nakasendo to the north of Ishida's castle of Ogaki. The period of the campaign that had been characterized by fighting for strongpoints therefore ended with the building of one. Construction began on 1 October to create a base not unlike an Ancient Roman *castrum*. Such places were not uncommon during large-scale campaigns, although contemporary records give few details of them. Far from being a simple curtained *maku* these positions, known as *jinya*, were formidable temporary constructions. We can have a good idea of the one at Akasaka from its inclusion on a contemporary painted screen in the possession of the Osaka City Museum of History, which shows it as a large-scale structure like a fortified town. A long curving ditch and embankment surrounds it, on top of which is a solid wooden palisade pierced by loopholes. Access is by means of a strong two-storey gatehouse and a wooden bridge. Inside the complex are barracks, storage posts and further enclosed areas, some surrounded by solid palisades, other just by the cloth *maku*. Hundreds of vertical *nobori* (long flags) hang in groups with *mon* (family crests) in common to show the location of the various daimyo, while the whole camp is packed with samurai and ashigaru (foot soldiers). Akasaka was indeed sufficiently strong to provide a secure base for the army over the next 19 days until Ieyasu came to join them.

Tokugawa Hidetada and the siege of Ueda

With the rival positions in Mino Province now more or less fixed and the base at Akasaka established, Ieyasu could consider moving his main body to the west from Edo. Date and Mogami were apparently containing Uesugi Kagekatsu, so the Tokugawa army departed. The first to leave was Hidetada, who departed from Utsunomiya for the mountain road on 1 October. This was to be the longer journey that this formidable father and son, travelling separately but attacking united, were to make, because unlike the friendly Tokaido the Nakasendo had at least one very serious nucleus of opposition at Ueda Castle, deep in the mountains of Shinano where the road turned south-west for the long descent towards Mino. Ueda held unpleasant memories for Ieyasu, because he had failed to capture it in 1586. The one great advantage possessed by the Tokugawa force with regard to Ueda was that the Sanada family who owned it were a house divided. The 1586 operation had resulted in a peace deal with Sanada Masayuki, one of the conditions being that he sent his eldest son Sanada Nobuyuki as hostage to the Tokugawa. Nobuyuki's sojourn with the Tokugawa was by no means unpleasant, and he married Komatsu-dono, the daughter of Tokugawa Ieyasu's famous retainer Honda Tadakatsu. From that time on Sanada Nobuyuki became a staunch Tokugawa supporter in direct opposition to the views of his father and his brother, whose stubbornness in opposition he deplored. The final split within the family occurred as the Sekigahara campaign was getting under way. Nobuyuki owned Numata Castle in Kozuke Province, and when Ieyasu issued the call to arms that was to lead to the decisive battle, Nobuyuki followed the Tokugawa while his father and brother in Ueda espoused the cause of Ishida Mitsunari. Just like Tomita in Anotsu Castle, Sanada Nobuyuki left Numata in the hands of his reliable wife Komatsu-dono when he set off to join Ieyasu. Very early in the campaign on 31 August the army of the other two Sanadas surrounded Numata. Komatsu-dono resolutely refused to surrender the castle or even to give admittance to her father-in-law, who expressed the desire to visit his grandchildren. Komatsu-dono was not fooled, and told him that if the Sanada army tried to force their way in she would burn the castle to the ground and commit suicide. Her defiance paid off and Sanada Masayuki and Yukimura withdrew to Ueda on the same day.

Sanada Nobuyuki had been allocated to Tokugawa Hidetada's Nakasendo army, which left Utsunomiya on 1 October. On 7 October they were at Karuizawa; two days later at Komoro and they came within sight of Ueda Castle on 11 October. There Hidetada proceeded to lay siege to the fortress in direct contravention of his father's orders. It was an error that could have cost the Tokugawa dear, because it was to mean that Hidetada missed the battle of Sekigahara, but when seen through Hidetada's eyes on 11 October one must have some sympathy for him in the difficult local decision he had to make. Ueda was formidable and had resisted the Tokugawa only 14 years earlier. How could Hidetada risk leaving such a hostile army at his rear, even if a masking force theoretically contained the castle? So he decided to capture it, and among the besiegers was Sanada Nobuyuki, who was concerned that many of the Sanada men who were with him had relatives inside the castle, a fact that was likely to affect their fighting spirit. In a brilliant move he and Komatsu-dono arranged for all non-combatants, such as wives, children and elderly parents, to be allowed to leave Ueda on humanitarian grounds and enter Numata Castle. It was an arrangement that suited both sides. On the Eastern side morale would be unaffected, and as the civilians included families affiliated to the pro-Ishida side of the family, Komatsu-dono's generous offer made them hostages while the siege continued. As for the defenders, they may have been thankful that there were fewer mouths

The yellow flag with crossed sickle *mon* (badge) of Kobayakawa Hideaki flies in front of Matsuoyama, the hill from which his samurai descended in the treacherous attack on Ishida Mitsunari's army that was to give Ieyasu his victory at Sekigahara.

This memorial marks the central point of the Sekigahara battlefield. Ishida Mitsunari's field headquarters lay on the hills to the rear. A banner bearing the Ishida *mon* flies beside two of the Tokugawa. Much of the area of the battlefield is well preserved and accessible.

to feed – always a consideration in battles of this sort. All these factors played a part in delaying Hidetada, who eventually abandoned his attempt at capturing Ueda on 16 October. Leaving a holding force behind him, he finally began the long descent towards Mino Province, but his progress was so slow that he had only reached the post-station of Magome on 21 October, the day of Sekigahara.

Tokugawa Hidetada could also have been stopped altogether a few miles further down the valley had it not been for the quick actions of a local Tokugawa supporter who recaptured his own family's former possession of Naegi, Japan's strangest-looking castle. Naegi Castle lay on a bluff overlooking the Kisogawa and the Nakasendo Road as it emerged from the mountainous centre of Japan near to modern Nakatsugawa. Naegi was of very curious appearance. Part of the hill on which it was built had been subject to the usual means of castle construction whereby the topsoil and vegetation were stripped away, sculpted and clad in stone, but the great central bulk of the mountain was a series of massive exposed boulders, which the original builder had ingeniously incorporated into the defences by surrounding them within an elaborate framework of jointed timber to make a massive platform upon which the keep sat. The grooves cut into the rocks to secure the supports are clearly visible today. Construction dated from the 1520s and for three generations it remained the possession of the Toyama family, only to be lost by them in 1582. It had eventually passed into the hands of Kawajiri Hidenaga of the Western Army. Control of Naegi, which was effectively the last castle before Gifu, could further frustrate the advance of Tokugawa Hidetada along the Nakasendo, so Ishida ordered its keeper Kawajiri Hidenaga to hold it at all costs. However, Naegi fell to an attack by a gleeful Toyama Tomomasa, the son of its former keeper, who was rewarded by Ieyasu after the campaign. Hidetada's army therefore passed the rocky pile of Naegi unmolested as they hurried down into the plains beyond, only to arrive at Ieyasu's camp at Sekigahara when the great battle was already over.

Ieyasu's march to Sekigahara

While Hidetada was sitting down in front of Ueda, Ieyasu was making his stately progress along the Tokaido. He had left Edo on 7 October, was at Odawara on 9 October, crossed the Hakone Pass below Mount Fuji to arrive at Mishima on 10 October, and was traversing the former Tokugawa provinces of Totomi and Mikawa when Mori Terumoto of the Western Army, fresh from his triumph at the taking of Anotsu, began an operation against the final significant Eastern possession at the western end of the Tokaido.

This was the castle of Otsu at the narrow neck of Lake Biwa. Near to it lay the Bridge of Seta, the symbolic river crossing that was Japan's Rubicon to poetically inclined samurai commanders, because having crossed the Bridge of Seta Kyoto was not far away. Since the loss of Fushimi, Otsu was the only Eastern possession near Kyoto, and was held stubbornly by Kyogoku Takatsugu, who came under attack on 13 October. The siege was still continuing two days later when Ieyasu reached his former childhood home of Okazaki. Tachibana Muneshige and Tsukushi Hirokado then joined Mori in the attempt on Otsu, all of which served to drain more and more Ishida supporters away from the crucial area near Ogaki where the coming showdown was looking increasingly inevitable. The Tachibana attack began on 19 October and was successfully concluded on 21 October, the day of the battle of Sekigahara. Kyogoku Takatsugu escaped to the sanctuary of Koyasan, where he was soon to receive the news that his garrison of 3,000 men had kept many times that number of enemies away from the decisive encounter.

At exactly the same time as the siege of Otsu was holding up Western troops, another Eastern Army supporter was making a nuisance of himself in the castle of Tanabe in Tango Province (modern Maizuru, Kyoto Prefecture) which lay to the north of the capital on the Sea of Japan. This man was Hosokawa Yusai Fujitaka, the father of Hosokawa Tadaoki. Very early in the campaign Tadaoki had gone off to join Ieyasu, leaving behind his wife, the celebrated and saintly Christian woman Gracia. We have heard twice already about women defending castles on behalf of absent husbands, but this was not to be the fate of poor Gracia. Instead Ishida's men surrounded her weakly defended mansion and demanded that she be taken to Osaka as a hostage. Tadaoki had been expecting such an eventuality and had ordered that if this course of action was imminent then his senior retainer was to put her to death, a fate Gracia meekly accepted. At this her father-in-law Hosokawa Yusai, by then aged 67 and a noted scholar and poet, shut himself up in Tanabe. A Western Army detachment of 15,000 men under the command of Onogi Shigekatsu marched from Fukuchiyama Castle in Tamba Province and

Ishida Mitsunari rides into action at Sekigahara in this modern painting in the Sekigahara Museum. Ieyasu's victory over him was partly due to treachery among Ishida's allies, but also owed a lot to Ieyasu's strategic vision that extended from one end of Japan to the other.

The death of Otani Yoshitsugu at the battle of Sekigahara is depicted in this section from a painted screen in the Watanabe Museum in Tottori. Otani received the full force of the treacherous attack by Kobayakawa Hideaki that changed the course of the battle. A sufferer from leprosy, Otani asked a retainer to put an end to him as he sat beside the palanquin in which he had to be carried.

began to besiege it on 28 August in one of the first actions of the Sekigahara War. The siege was still continuing two days before the battle of Sekigahara; a prolonged 50-day operation that had a lot to do with the fact that Hosokawa Yusai was so beloved as a scholar that the besieging army had no wish to hurt him. We are told that some cannon were fired at the castle with no cannonballs inside them, and the surrender of Tanabe, which came about on 19 October too late to allow Onogi to reach Sekigahara, was itself a protracted affair of negotiations involving imperial representatives and guarantees of safe conduct, not only for the poet himself but for all the books in his library.

On 19 October Tokugawa Ieyasu, guarded by the friendly castles his loyal vanguard had secured for him and having branched off north from the Tokaido, arrived at Gifu. If the other major element in his plans had gone smoothly Hidetada would probably have been waiting for him there, but his son was still negotiating the valley roads. So the following day, Ieyasu made a grand entrance to the fortified encampment of Akasaka, much to the astonishment of Ishida and his allies, who had expected him to be so beset by Uesugi Kagekatsu that he not dared leave Edo. Uesugi Kagekatsu (or at least his local supporters, because Kagekatsu never left Wakamatsu during the entire Tohoku Sekigahara campaign) had indeed been very active but was countered all along the line in a series of holding operations similar to the defence of Otsu but on a much large scale, as will be described later.

The battle of Kuisegawa

When the news of Ieyasu's arrival at Akasaka reached Ogaki Castle the Western leaders called a hasty council of war. What, precisely, were Ieyasu's intentions? Was he going to attack Ogaki? Was he going to march further along and capture Ishida's home castle of Sawayama? Was he even going to ignore both places and direct his mighty army against Osaka? While they debated about what was really happening and what should be their immediate response, only one among them actually suggested attacking Tokugawa Ieyasu's army. This bold suggestion was made by Shimazu Yoshihiro, the daimyo of Satsuma Province (modern Kagoshima Prefecture in Kyushu), who offered to lead the operation along with his nephew Yoshihisa. Shimazu had reconnoitred the position at Akasaka and found some of the Eastern Army exhausted and asleep in their armour. But Ishida did not agree. Mentally he was already on the way to take up the positions that would begin the battle of Sekigahara, so the only action carried out on

20 October was led by Shima Sakon, who held the rank of *samurai-taisho* (general of samurai) in Ishida Mitsunari's army. He had not supported a full-scale attack on the well-defended camp at Akasaka, but thought that an immediate engagement would not only test their opponents' strength but also bolster the morale of the Western Army. Ieyasu had wisely placed the Kuisegawa between his fortified camp and Ogaki Castle, so Ishida gave Shima permission to carry out a raid across the river. This he did accompanied by Gamo Hideyuki and 500 men at a place called Ikejiri, leaving other troops behind as an ambush. Shima hoped to tempt the Eastern Army into making an attack and be lured across the river, so his party pretended to begin harvesting rice. Nakamura Kazuuji was the Eastern commander nearest to the scene, and one of his officers, Noisshiki Tanomo, took the bait only to be counterattacked as soon as he had crossed in pursuit of the false retreat, just as Shima had planned. Shima Sakon took about 140 heads, which he gleefully displayed at Ogaki, but the short battle

The retreat from Sekigahara by the Shimazu family of Satsuma is shown here in this section from a painted screen in the Watanabe Museum in Tottori. The reluctance of the Shimazu to engage in battle and their rapid fighting retreat when they felt the day was lost contributed greatly to Ishida Mitsunari's defeat by Tokugawa Ieyasu.

of Kuisegawa, the curtain-raiser to Sekigahara, turned out to be the only victory that the Western troops were to gain. It is interesting to note that the action was fought sufficiently close to Ieyasu's quarters that he was able to watch the fight from the roof while dining. Attendants helpfully placed boards along the roof so that he could enjoy the action, where he became so engrossed in the spectacle that he dropped some rice from his chopsticks. He commended Nakamura's handling of troops, but observed that it was a mistake for him to cross the river in pursuit.

It was at this precise moment that Ishida Mitsunari made the most important decision of his career. He had concluded that Ieyasu would move on and had to be stopped. Ishida also knew the best place to do it, so the majority of his army would leave Ogaki and march about 15km westwards to join the Nakasendo at a place where his good eye for strategy had told him that Ieyasu's advance against Sawayama could

The charge of the Red Devils of the Ii family at the battle of Sekigahara is shown in this section of a painted screen in the Sekigahara Warland Museum. The screen is modern and based on the better-known version in Nagoya. To the right Ieyasu's *maku* (field curtains) may be seen.

not only be halted but destroyed in battle. It lay where the ground was defined by the hills around a village called Sekigahara.

It was a dark and damp evening in October when Ishida marched out to take up a position across paddy fields from which the rice had been harvested but were now wet from the rain. To the casual eye the image of Ishida Mitsunari marching to his doom at Sekigahara looks like a retreat, but the Western Army was not going to Sekigahara just to form neat ranks across an undefended front. Ishida had made plans, and just as the Eastern Army had built their fortified camp at Akasaka, so had the Westerners at Sekigahara. On the hills around, cleared of foliage for much of their area, stood field defences surrounded by ditches and palisades. They were not as extensive as Akasaka but were sturdy enough to provide a welcome for the Western Army and, for its senior members at least, a dry mat to sleep on during the short night. Seven thousand five hundred men were left behind under Fukuhara Nagataka to defend Ogaki Castle, which was indeed to come under attack when the field battle began.

Of all the fortified camps that were established at Sekigahara the strongest was that on Matsuoyama where Kobayakawa Hideaki had arrived during the day of 20 October. His men had quickly cleared the ground and put up rudimentary palisades. Ishida Mitsunari's position was also on a hill nearer to the roads and was defended by loose palisades of sharpened stakes, bundles of bamboo, and a crude abattis made from felled trees. There they waited for Ieyasu's attack.

The battle of Sekigahara

When General Meckel, a Prussian military advisor to the Meiji government, was shown a plan of the Western Army's dispositions prior to the battle of Sekigahara, he is said to have exclaimed, 'They must have won!', because Ishida Mitsunari's formation so impressed him. Ishida's forces were arranged in the *kakuyoku* (crane's wing) formation, one of a number of traditional battle layouts associated with the Emperor Taizong of the Tang dynasty of China, and one recommended as a good means of absorbing an attack. The centre companies would do this, and then the wings of the crane would fold around the attacking enemy.

At Sekigahara a road left the Nakasendo for the north to head round Lake Biwa and on to Wakasa Province (modern Fukui Prefecture). This created a fork, so the centre of the Western Army lay on the flat ground or lowest part of the hills just to the west of the fork. The largest contingent there was Ukita Hideie (17,000) with Konishi Yukinaga (4,000) on his left. Ishida Mitsunari (6,000) formed the largest contingent in the left wing of the crane north of the spur road on Sasaoyama. In front of him were Shima Sakon and Gamo Hideyuki. The south wing of the crane, below the Nakasendo, was formed by Otani Yoshitsugu (3,500) while behind him was the very large contingent under Kobayakawa Hideaki (15,600). There was also a large detached force under Mori Hidemoto and others (15,000) quite a distance away near modern Tarui to the east of the main body up on Nanguyama to the south of the Nakasendo, who were ready to fall on Ieyasu's rear.

So how did Ieyasu deal with this potential death trap? The answer is that he marched straight into it, relying first on his loyal followers to absorb whatever punishment the Western Army could give them, but gambling most on the assurance he had been given that certain of Ishida's followers intended to change sides once the battle had begun. The most important among these was Kobayakawa Hideaki on Matsuoyama, whose role as Ishida's second wave for a flank attack would be crucial, and his kinsmen from the extended family of the Mori – Mori Hidemoto and Kikkawa Hiroie – who were supposedly waiting to attack Ieyasu in the rear.

With these thoughts in mind Tokugawa Ieyasu's army set out from Akasaka at 3am on 21 October. Unlike the Westerners, his men did not take up entrenched positions but moved into battle formation on a narrow front. Six contingents made up the front ranks, and at about 8am they stood very close to the Western forward units. From north to south the Eastern Army vanguard was Kuroda Nagamasa, Hosokawa Tadaoki, Kato Yoshiaki, Tsutsui Sadatsugu and Tanaka Yoshimasa, with the largest unit in the vanguard, that of Fukushima Masanori with 6,000 men, being somewhat in advance of them and exactly in front of Ukita Hideie's position. Just behind Fukushima were Kyogoku Takatomo and Todo Takatora, who were also to attack towards the centre of the crane, totally ignoring the threat to their left wing that Ieyasu hoped was non-existent.

Ieyasu's parting words on leaving Akasaka are supposed to have been, 'For us there are only two alternatives, either to come back with a bloody

This shrine on the site of the battlefield of Sekigahara marks the mound of the Eastern Army heads, reverently interred here after the battle.

head in our hands or to leave our own for the enemy.' With this he rode off with his personal contingent of 30,000 troops into the dark and the damp fog. He set up his first field position somewhat to the rear at Momokubariyama, an auspicious location as it had been the site of a victorious ancient general's camp in AD 672.

Even though Fukushima Masanori had been selected as the Eastern vanguard and was further forward than any other contingent he was not

43

The battle of Sekigahara, 1600

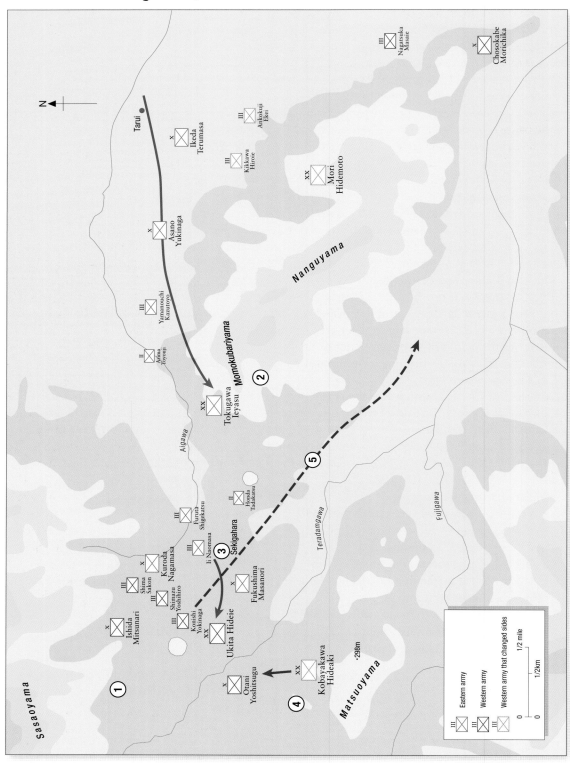

to earn the great glory of being first into battle, because as he dressed his ranks and awaited the order to engage, a commotion to his rear heralded the surprise advance of Ii Naomasa, who had been placed in the second rank and was thereby mortified. Accompanied by the troops of Ieyasu's fourth son, Matsudaira Tadayoshi, Ii took the chance of gaining much renown and simply raced past Fukushima into the attack. Thus it was that the first shots of the battle of Sekigahara were exchanged between the 'Red Devils' of Ii and Ukita Hideie's men. Needless to say, Fukushima Masanori quickly joined them in the centre, while the above-mentioned units of the Eastern vanguard engaged Shima, Gamo and Konishi in a massive and indecisive series of melees. A second wave of Easterners under Terazawa Hirotaka brought fresh impetus to the attack on Konishi Yukinaga, whose formation began to collapse. At this point the first suspicions of reluctance on the part of his supposed comrades began to enter Ishida Mitsunari's mind, because Shimazu Yoshihiro, who was located to the left of Konishi Yukinaga and somewhat to his rear, had not yet engaged and showed no inclination of so doing. Others were totally committed, particularly the Otani father and son of Yoshitsugu and Yoshikatsu, who stood on either side of the Nakasendo and advanced into action to drive back the Eastern advance against their front.

It was time for Ishida Mitsunari to bring into action the large force that made up his right wing to deliver the decisive blow to the Tokugawa eastern flank. This was Kobayakawa Hideaki on Matsuoyama, which was a considerable distance away, so it had been agreed that he would join the battle when he saw the plume of smoke from a signal fire lit above Ishida's headquarters. The fire was ignited, but there was no movement on Matsuoyama. Otani and Konishi, who both needed his help, sent horseback messengers to him but still no reinforcement materialized. Tokugawa Ieyasu, meanwhile, was also becoming concerned, because the assurance he had been given was not merely that Kobayakawa would do nothing but that he would actually change sides. So Ieyasu ordered his men to approach and open fire on Kobayakawa's position. This proved to be the decisive stimulus he needed, and his troops started to descend Matsuoyama and move across to attack Otani Yoshitsugu. The delay in Kobayakawa committing himself however had allowed the

Uesugi Kagekatsu was Ieyasu's chief opponent in the Tohoku (north-east) region and thus had the ability to threaten Ieyasu's provinces while he was engaged in the west of Japan. Fortunately the skills of Ieyasu's allies neutralized Uesugi's opposition.

Opposite:
1. Ishida Mitsunari leaves Ogaki Castle and takes up a prepared position below Sasaoyama.
2. Tokugawa leaves Akasaka Jinya and takes up his first position beneath Momokubariyama.
3. Ii Naomasa passes Fukushima Masanori to open the attack against Ukita Hideie.
4. Kobayakawa Hideaki launches a treacherous attack against Otani.
5. Shimazu breaks out of the battle and causes consternation to the troops on Nanguyama.

suspicious Otani ample time to prepare, so he had rearranged his ranks and drove back the treacherous assault. But it was not only Kobayakawa Hideaki on the right wing of the crane that changed sides but every other contingent there except Otani himself and Kinoshita, leaving Otani isolated and attacked on all sides. As a sufferer from leprosy he had to be carried in a palanquin, out of which he leaned and asked an attendant to kill him and hide his head. This the man did, and with that the resistance on the right wing of the Western Army faded to nothing. Ukita and Konishi now discovered that they were being attacked in the rear as well as from an advancing front. Shimazu Yoshihiro alone was left, but he had no stomach for a fight, and when many of his men were cut down he led a desperate charge forward, not to engage with the Eastern Army but to break through them to escape along the road to the coast of Ise Province and eventually back to the safety of distant Satsuma. Ii Naomasa was determined to take Shimazu's head, but as he pursued him a musketeer, left behind among the rearguard, discharged his weapon and wounded Ii Naomasa in the elbow.

By now Ishida and Konishi had also fled, leaving their allies to their fate. All that remained of the Western Army were the detached units on Nanguyama. Two of them, Nagatsuka Masaie and Ankokuji Ekei, had been inclined to join in the fighting, but were reluctant to move their men when Kikkawa Hiroie in the vanguard of this unit was doing nothing. Soon they saw a charge coming towards them, but it was not an attack. Instead it was the remnants of Shimazu Yoshihiro's army heading for home. So Nagatsuka Masaie and Chosokabe Morichika withdrew along with them, as did Mori's huge contingent.

By 2pm Ieyasu was sufficiently confident that the day was his that he began to prepare for the head-viewing ceremony; so he took off the light cloth hood that he had been wearing and put on his helmet for the first time in the battle. The memory of the death of his former overlord Imagawa Yoshimoto in

similar circumstances 40 years earlier must still have been a vivid one, so his comment, 'after a victory tighten the cords of your helmet', was to become a Japanese proverb. His exhausted troops had more pressing concerns such as how to find nourishment. The rain prevented cooking fires from being lit so the soldiers soaked raw rice in water before eating it as it was.

A mopping-up operation for survivors then began, but there were still some fortified positions to secure. One, the castle of Mizoguchi to which Nagatsuka Masaie had fled, was secured for Ieyasu by the simple means of sending a messenger ordering Nagatsuka to commit suicide, which he eventually did on 5 November. The other place was Ogaki Castle, which stubbornly refused to surrender for another two days in spite of the defeat at Sekigahara that had happened on its doorstep. The siege of Ogaki, an action totally overshadowed by the victory at Sekigahara, was a considerable operation for which we have an unusual eyewitness in the form of a diary written by Oan the daughter of Yamada Koreyuki, one of the defenders. She describes the horrors of living under bombardment, both from the noise of their own cannon as well as that of the shot from the enemy, and how she and the other women of the garrisons were busy casting bullets in moulds or preparing the heads of enemy soldiers for presentation. Eventually Oan escaped when an arrow letter was fired into Ogaki assuring Yamada Koreyuki, a former teacher of Ieyasu, that he would not be harmed. He and his daughter then climbed down a pine tree over the wall to escape.

The Tohoku Sekigahara campaign

The campaign in Tohoku whereby Uesugi Kagekatsu was neutralized provides the best example of the trust as a commander Ieyasu placed in his allies and subordinates. Date Masamune played an active role in the initial stages. Mogami Yoshiaki was fully involved throughout. Their opponent, Uesugi Kagekatsu, delegated the entire conduct of the campaign to others, in particular Naoe Kanetsugu, a brilliant general who organized three separate armies to move against Mogami's castle of Yamagata. His main body of 20,000 men circled round to approach from the west while his second division of 4,000 men under Hommura Chikamori headed against the castle of Kaminoyama to the south of Yamagata, which was held by Satomi Minbu. Meanwhile a third army approached from Shonai to the north of Yamagata.

Naoe Kanetsugu's main body encountered their first obstacle in the form of the castle of Hataya, defended by the redoubtable Eguchi Gohei. As soon as word was brought to him of the advance of Kanetsugu's army he gave orders for the ditches to be deepened and walls to be strengthened. His garrison were determined fighters, and morale was helped during the attack when a *ninja* infiltrated the Naoe camp and brought back a battle flag, which was then flown in mockery from the main gate. Naoe Kanetsugu eventually triumphed owing to sheer weight of numbers, because Eguchi's garrison was only 300 strong.

A short march eastwards the following day placed the Naoe army in a position from which they could threaten the castle of Hasedo, the last Mogami outpost before Yamagata, where Naoe settled down for a siege. Hasedo was certainly larger than Hataya, but his lack of urgency suggests that Kanetsugu was unaware that the Mogami

Kato Kiyomasa was one of the mainstays of the Kyushu Sekigahara campaign. His operations were directed against his rival Konishi Yukinaga.

47

and Date forces had been shadowing his moves, and were almost ready to close in. Over the following 15 days its commander bought time for Date and Mogami as he waged a war of attrition against the besiegers.

Date Masamune had delegated the command of his army to his uncle Date Masakage, and the two commands joined forces to the east of Hasedo. On learning of their approach Naoe Kanetsugu ordered an all-out attack on the castle. His vanguard under Kasuga Mototada fought bravely but was stopped at the castle's outer defences by fierce harquebus fire. Kanetsugu then ordered a tactical withdrawal, but as this was happening a sortie was made from the castle that caught the Naoe army in the rear. Naoe Kanetsugu, for all his bravery, was in a very difficult position, but the issue was not going to be resolved by a battle in Tohoku, because while Kanetsugu was on his fighting retreat northwards on 5 November a courier guard arrived from Uesugi Kagekatsu with some very serious news. The coalition under Ishida Mitsunari to which they belonged had been defeated at a place called Sekigahara. It may not have been appreciated then just how serious the news was, but the guardsman ordered Naoe Kanetsugu to retreat to Yonezawa and safety. The Date and Mogami also heard the news about Sekigahara at about the same time, and redoubled their efforts to catch Kanetsugu before he could withdraw. His rearguard was harassed as he moved south, eventually arriving at Uesugi Kagekatsu's castle of Aizu-Wakamatsu to have it confirmed that all their plans had come to nothing.

The Kyushu Sekigahara campaign

The Kyushu Sekigahara campaign saw the rivalry between Tokugawa Ieyasu and Ishida Mitsunari being fought out by their supporters in southern Japan. The main player on the Tokugawa side here was Kuroda Josui Yoshitaka, the father of Kuroda Nagamasa who fought at Sekigahara. First of all Josui went to the castle of Kitsuke on the Kunisaki Peninsula in modern Oita Prefecture, from where his first taste of action occurred some time after Sekigahara when his ships encountered a fleet of ships taking the Shimazu back to

Tokugawa Ieyasu, in supreme command at the battle of Sekigahara in 1600, watches the advance of the Ii family

It is now Ieyasu's hour of destiny at Sekigahara. Gone are the days when he would take the head of his army when a battle began. Instead we see merely an indication of his presence vaguely through the fog and rain in the background, surrounded by his bodyguards. Only the great golden sun standard and the ever-present Jodo banner confirm his presence on the battlefield amid the darkness. Yet his hand has been everywhere in the planning and execution of this huge and meticulous campaign, including placing in the vanguard his loyal follower Ii Naomasa, whose 'Red Devils' in their brightly lacquered armour add a splash of colour to the scene. Every man in this division is dressed in red, and above them flies the Ii battle flag with the gold character from their name on a huge red field. Ii Naomasa's armour is preserved in Hikone Castle Museum.

Kagoshima. Josui then began an attack by land to take the nearby castles of the remaining Ishida supporters.

Josui's greatest ally over on the western coast of Kyushu was Kato Kiyomasa of Kumamoto. When the decisive campaign of 1600 was launched Tokugawa Ieyasu advised Kato, who had declared his support for the Tokugawa cause, that he would best serve their interests not by making a long journey to Central Japan but by staying in Kyushu and attacking the anti-Tokugawa fiefs of Higo and Chikugo, which would then be given to him as a reward. This Kato rushed to do, and 23 October was to find him on his way from Higo to the Kunisaki Peninsula on the opposite coast of Kyushu to assist Josui in the vanquishing of Otomo Yoshimune. On that day Kiyomasa was informed that Kuroda Josui had achieved a victory at Ishigakihara two days earlier (on 21 October, the same day as Sekigahara) so he rapidly doubled back and attacked Konishi Yukinaga's domains instead. By now Konishi Yukinaga had been captured at Sekigahara and was to be executed shortly afterwards, but Yukinaga's kinsmen put up a fierce resistance. Konishi Yashichiro Hayato, Yukinaga's son-in-law from the Hibiya family, defended Uto Castle valiantly but ultimately unsuccessfully, but Kato Kiyomasa generously let people escape from the castle in return for Yashichiro committing suicide. When the news of the fall of Uto was brought to him, Konishi Yukishige fled from the besieged Yatsushiro Castle and the ruin of Konishi Yukinaga was complete.

Tachibana Muneshige, the daimyo of Yanagawa Castle who had captured Otsu Castle, was another supporter of Ishida Mitsunari who fled back to Kyushu after Sekigahara to seek refuge. Ieyasu sent Nabeshima Katsushige, Kuroda Josui and Kato Kiyomasa after him, and the resulting military action was to provide a unique example of a variation on the familiar theme of warrior monks in the person of Ginchiyo, the warrior nun of Yanagawa, because the castle's defence was helped by the presence of a small defended strongpoint to the south in the shape of the convent where Tachibana Muneshige's divorced wife, Ginchiyo, now resided. In an act of surprising loyalty to her ex-husband Ginchiyo organized her fellow nuns in armed resistance against the advancing army of Kato Kiyomasa, who was proceeding from the south. We know very little about the actual defensive measures adopted by Ginchiyo. Her resistance may only have been one of dressing up in armour and looking defiant, but it seems to have made the point. Kuroda and Kato were old comrades-in-arms of Tachibana Muneshige from the days of the Korean invasion, and following the unexpected resistance by Ginchiyo they proposed that he should surrender and join them in a campaign against the Shimazu, who had also fled from Sekigahara. Muneshige agreed, but Ieyasu ordered the campaign to stop almost before it had begun because he did not want a further war in Kyushu. Tachibana Muneshige was pardoned nonetheless.

Epilogue at Osaka

With the conclusion of the Kyushu Sekigahara campaign Ieyasu's hour of destiny was complete. In the immediate aftermath of Sekigahara there was little opposition left to prevent Tokugawa Ieyasu taking the title he desired.

He was formally proclaimed shogun in 1603, and set in motion a number of schemes to consolidate his family's position. These included a massive redistribution of domains so that those who had opposed Ieyasu at Sekigahara by word or deed found themselves being moved to the far corners of Japan. Needless to say, this provoked great resentment among the losers in the process, and the greatest loser of all was Hideyori, the heir of Toyotomi Hideyoshi, who had been disinherited by Ieyasu's victory. Since the time of Sekigahara, Toyotomi Hideyori had been a virtual prisoner in Osaka Castle, but the process of land transfer and punishment of opponents of the Tokugawa between 1603 and 1614 threw on to the military stage many thousands of *ronin* (masterless samurai) who found in Toyotomi Hideyori a focus for their resentment against Ieyasu. These men and their dispossessed lords packed themselves into Osaka Castle, forcing the Tokugawa to march against them. The Winter Campaign, as it was called, involved attacks on the huge fortress and also the deployment by the Tokugawa of terrible new weapons in the form of European cannon with ranges much longer than the

The Ii family were among the most loyal supporters of Tokugawa Ieyasu. Ii Naomasa fought at Sekigahara and was wounded there. His son Ii Naotaka served during the Osaka campaign, and is shown here leading a charge against Kimura Shigenari's army at the battle of Wakae, an unsuccessful attempt to head off the Tokugawa army. The Ii samurai are shown in their characteristic red-lacquered armour in this section of a painted screen in Hikone Castle Museum.

simple breech-loaders possessed by the defenders. A few well-aimed shots into the keep drove the Toyotomi family to the negotiation table, where Ieyasu's cunning and blatant lies persuaded the garrison to fill in the outer moat and demolish the outer walls. As some had rightly feared, Tokugawa Ieyasu returned in the summer of 1615, and with the castle at his mercy the defending armies under Hideyori's skilled general Sanada Yukimura chose to advance and fight Ieyasu and his son on the flatland of Tennoji. This was to be the final Tokugawa victory, but for many hours the outcome was in doubt. Eventually the defenders succumbed and the castle was burned. Toyotomi Hideyori committed suicide, thereby leaving no figurehead for any future opposition to a Tokugawa hegemony that was to last for another two and a half centuries. His work completed, Tokugawa Ieyasu died peacefully in bed in the following year of 1616, his hands clutching a sword.

OPPOSING COMMANDERS

During key campaigns in his career Tokugawa Ieyasu came up against several very different commanders, each of whom was to expose Ieyasu's strengths and weaknesses in various ways. The four most important are discussed here.

Takeda Shingen

Takeda Shingen had such confidence in the loyalty of his samurai and the difficulties posed by the natural barrier of the mountains of Kai that he never erected a castle, ruling his domain instead from the splendid moated mansion of Tsutsujigasaki. By the time young Tokugawa Ieyasu came on to the scene, Shingen had already fought five battles against his great rival Uesugi Kenshin at Kawanakajima (modern Matsushiro, Nagano Prefecture). The battle of Mikatagahara in 1572 therefore pitted the old and experienced Takeda Shingen against the young and impetuous Tokugawa Ieyasu, a man who had yet to learn the virtue of patience that would ultimately make him shogun. Mikatagahara presents an example of a field battle from prearranged positions, several instances of personal bravery, an epic retreat and some very subtle psychological warfare that finally saved the day for Tokugawa Ieyasu. Yet by all accounts Mikatagahara should not have been fought at all. Ieyasu's closest followers advised against it, and the progress of the battle until the retreat seemed to confirm their worst suspicions. Compared with Takeda Shingen's tactical vision on the day, Ieyasu comes out of the encounter very badly as a field commander. To leave the security of one's castle as night was about to fall was an act of incredible recklessness, and the house of Tokugawa could well have been extinguished that very afternoon. Yet intelligence is one of the martial virtues, and the way Ieyasu acted so calmly and so deliberately following the retreat shows him in a very good light as one who understood the importance of psychological warfare. If one is to be even more generous to Ieyasu, then perhaps he appreciated that Shingen was unlikely to begin a siege as winter was commencing. Indeed, was Shingen at fault for marching out of Kai at that time of the year? As the years went by Ieyasu was to prove time and again that he could out-think his opponents even if he could not always outfight them, so we may well regard Mikatagahara as Tokugawa Ieyasu's most successful defeat.

Toyotomi Hideyoshi

Toyotomi Hideyoshi was to be Ieyasu's most formidable opponent during the whole of his career, and it is evident that Ieyasu had such respect for him that he avoided any clash of interests as much as possible. Until Oda Nobunaga's death in 1582 each had operated in different areas of Japan on Nobunaga's directions. Being unable to take any meaningful part in the subsequent destruction of Akechi Mitsuhide at Yamazaki, Ieyasu had waited on the sidelines, busying himself in the administration of the former Takeda provinces of Kai and Shinano that he had

Takeda Shingen was one of the most formidable opponents that Ieyasu encountered during his long military career, defeating him at the battle of Mikatagahara in 1572. In this cartoon-like print we see Takeda Shingen at the second battle of Kawanakajima in 1555.

received from Nobunaga as a reward. This also involved absorbing into his army many hundreds of former Takeda retainers, so his military resources were considerable. In 1583 Ieyasu also avoided getting involved in the Shizugatake campaign whereby Hideyoshi secured Nobunaga's inheritance, but he was a daimyo of five provinces that were now close to Hideyoshi's domains, and it was clearly only a matter of time before their spheres of influence collided. At that time the provinces they controlled were divided from one another by Owari, the home of Oda Nobuo, who was to play a major role in matters as they unfolded in 1584.

The Komaki–Nagakute campaign is one that reflects well on both commanders. Both sensibly used their experience of Nagashino to erect field fortifications, but then the samurai spirit asserted itself by the decision to relieve boredom by fighting a battle somewhere else. In this Ieyasu was initially completely outmanoeuvred by Hideyoshi, who managed to detach an army from the lines at Komaki without Ieyasu realizing it. The subsequent manoeuvres over the next 24 hours prior to the battle of Nagakute are fascinating, and depended totally on the fact that an advancing column occupied a great deal of space. Yet each reacted coolly to often baffling intelligence reports. The subsequent stand-off lasted for several months, but from the end of 1584 the relations between Ieyasu and Hideyoshi changed from military campaigning to politics. Each came to see that the other was worth more with a head than without one, so Ieyasu submitted. Hideyoshi, he reasoned, could not last forever, and between them they could conquer the rest of Japan.

Hideyoshi's gift to Ieyasu of the Kanto provinces of the Hojo following their defeat at Odawara finally demonstrated the control Hideyoshi had over him, because Ieyasu left the provinces with which he had been

Ishida Mitsunari was one of Hideyoshi's most accomplished generals who served with distinction at the siege of Oshi in 1590 and during the Korean invasion. He is of course best remembered for being the loser to Tokugawa Ieyasu at the decisive battle of Sekigahara in 1600.

associated since birth. He nevertheless treated the whole process in a very positive manner, choosing Edo, now the great city of Tokyo, for his capital rather than Odawara, but the element of control present in an apparent reward for good behaviour is very evident. The move shifted the Tokugawa responsibilities further to the east, thus allowing more scope for Hideyoshi to consolidate his position. Once again these two military giants moved away from each other, and Ieyasu was to avoid any involvement in Hideyoshi's wars for the rest of the latter's life.

Ishida Mitsunari

Ieyasu's avoidance of service in Korea left him in a very strong position when Hideyoshi died, and when conflict came in 1600 Ieyasu found that he was opposing not one strong man but a loose coalition under Ishida Mitsunari, a fine general in his own right but one who was lacking in the political skills needed to bind the alliance in a genuine commitment to the cause of Hideyori. Ishida Mitsunari was born in Omi Province, and had first come to Hideyoshi's attention as a youth because of his prowess at the tea ceremony. He soon proved to be an excellent general, and earned great admiration from Hideyoshi when he captured the fortress of Oshi during the 1590 campaign against the Hojo. Oshi lay in low-lying ground, so Ishida paid Hideyoshi the compliment of using his master's favourite siege technique of building an embankment and then flooding the castle. Ishida Mitsunari then served in Korea with some distinction, so it is unfortunate for him that he is best remembered for being defeated by Ieyasu at his most crucial battle. Here Ishida was his weakest opponent, and Ieyasu played him like a fish on a line. Yet Sekigahara was no pushover. Everything depended on the willingness of certain Western commanders to change sides, and if Ishida had not lost his right wing the outcome could have been very different.

Sanada Yukimura

Although the Osaka campaign of 1614–15 was nominally in the hands of Ieyasu's son Tokugawa Hidetada who became shogun in 1605, Ieyasu was so closely involved with all the decisions made that he was still effectively in command of the Tokugawa army. In that capacity he encountered one of the most skilled and challenging opposing commanders of his career. Sanada Yukimura was the brother of Sanada Nobuyuki who had become a loyal Tokugawa supporter. After Sekigahara and the siege of Ueda Nobuyuki was given the Sanada territories in Shinano and Yukimura was sent into exile as a monk on Koyasan. He returned from there in 1614 to command the Osaka garrison on behalf of Toyotomi Hideyori, and the way he led the defence speaks volumes about his skills as a commander and his unquenchable loyalty to Hideyori, a factor that put to shame many who had fought for that same cause at Sekigahara. He supervised the construction of the Sanada barbican that extended the defences of Osaka, and then opposed the surrender negotiations that led to the weakening of the defences in 1615. When the final battle came he led the Toyotomi army in the battle of Tennoji, which placed the Tokugawa family in a situation of greater peril even than at Sekigahara. At Tennoji Ieyasu was challenged as a general more severely than he had been since Nagakute, and a strong local tradition even has Sanada Yukimura fighting Ieyasu in single combat and killing him, so that for the rest of his life the part of Ieyasu was played by a double!

INSIDE THE MIND

In the person of Tokugawa Ieyasu Japan completed the transition from the Medieval to the Early Modern Period. His great predecessor Toyotomi Hideyoshi may have reunified Japan and through that process ended forever the medieval patchwork of petty daimyo in favour of a single united Japanese state, but the Toyotomi hegemony turned out to be a house built upon sand. The successful Tokugawa regime was built upon a rock, and that rock was Ieyasu. Whereas the Toyotomi regime collapsed within two years of Hideyoshi's death and the accession of his five-year-old son Toyotomi Hideyori, the Tokugawa family endured for two and a half centuries until Japan entered the modern world. As it was Ieyasu who brought about his rival's collapse, the contrasting images of the wily old Tokugawa Ieyasu and

Tokugawa Ieyasu's statue appears here in the Buddhist temple of Daijuji in Okazaki. This was the *bodaiji* (family temple) of the Matsudaira family.

the youthful Toyotomi Hideyori inevitably call to mind the old Chinese saying: If a rock falls upon an egg; alas for the egg; if an egg falls upon a rock, alas for the egg!

Tokugawa Ieyasu's undoubted achievements as a statesman and a politician have tended to obscure his record as a commander. The above accounts of his battles have set out his generalship skills, yet Ieyasu's career resembled that of a cat with nine lives. The first of his nine lives was to have survived childhood as a hostage. As a young man he was forced to fight for his overlord Imagawa Yoshimoto in one of the greatest defeats in Japanese history. Ieyasu's third life was lost when he went into battle on his own account against the Buddhist armies of the Ikko-ikki in 1564 and received bullets in his shirt. His fourth life expired at the battle of Mikatagahara in 1572 when, instead of staying safely in Hamamatsu Castle he marched out to give battle, only to be ignominiously defeated and chased home. In 1584, confronting the mighty Toyotomi Hideyoshi from field defences at Komaki, he allowed himself to be outflanked so much that his own province was raided behind his back, his fifth life. In 1590 he took part in what was likely to be a major bloodbath with the siege of the Hojo's castle of Odawara, only to see it surrender peacefully. With six lives gone Ieyasu cleverly avoided sending any troops to Hideyoshi's disaster in Korea, claiming that his distance from the port of embarkation made it impossible. In his decisive victory at Sekigahara, Tokugawa Ieyasu risked everything and might have lost. The cat had used up eight of his nine lives. The final one was placed in the balance during the summer campaign of Osaka in 1615, when the siege was finally resolved in the last great field encounter between two samurai armies. The outrageous alternative version of the Osaka campaign tells us that Tokugawa Ieyasu was actually killed there and that his place was taken by a *kagemusha* (substitute) but his nine lives officially ran out when he died in bed the following year.

Luck aside, the essence of Ieyasu's abilities and success lay in his unparalleled personal combination of the two virtues stressed by all his contemporaries yet so rarely demonstrated by anyone else. These were *bun* and *bu*, the civil and the military arts. Ieyasu was a good swordsman, a fine horseman, a keen archer and a strong swimmer, and was also accomplished in the art of musketry, which many of his contemporaries affected to despise as being the military art of the lower orders. He kept fit by hunting and hawking, two pursuits that he enjoyed until late in life. *Shogi* (Japanese chess) and the other popular board game of *go* amused him from time to time, although it would be going too far to suggest that either affected his tactical or strategic thinking. Like most samurai he was a connoisseur of swords, and prized highly any rare ones that were presented to him in recognition of his services on the battlefield.

We have also noted above a certain recklessness in his youth when battle was actually joined. In later life he commented that battles were never won by sitting on a camp stool, command baton in hand, gazing at the backs of one's soldiers; victory could better be gained by charging with great vigour.

This may have been an ironic statement, because he never behaved like this again after nearly dying at Mikatagahara.

Religion always seems to have sat lightly upon him, and Ieyasu approached spiritual matters from the point of view of pragmatism rather than committed belief. Ieyasu belonged to the Jodo (Pure Land) sect of Buddhism and treasured a banner presented to him by the chief priest of a temple in Okazaki. It bore the slogan, 'Renounce this Filthy World and Attain the Pure Land' and was carried at all his battles. The rival True Pure Land sect was an offshoot of Jodo and had caused much trouble in his younger days through their Ikko-ikki armies, so when the opportunity arose to curtail any revival of them as a military force Ieyasu took it. Hideyoshi had destroyed them militarily, and early in Ieyasu's reign a succession dispute within the sect allowed him to divide it into two. Ieyasu's attitude towards death in battle was one of acceptance that it could happen, and he impressed upon his followers that they must accept such a fate to the extent of urging them to burn incense inside their helmets so that their head might present a more attractive trophy when severed.

As for Japan's other great religion of Shinto, Ieyasu honoured the *kami* (deities) of his locality and his family, and after death was to be honoured himself as a very great *kami* – Tosho Daigongen, 'the great avatar of the sun god of the east'. Yet by far the greatest religious influence on him was Confucianism with its vision of a harmonious and ordered society where everyone knew their place; where the lord received loyalty to the point of death (a dedication exemplified for the Tokugawa by the behaviour of Torii Mototada at Fushimi) and the lord responded with benevolence.

Ieyasu possessed the particular gift of divining who should be an ally and who was an enemy, and he also was an expert in the broad-brush strokes of a campaign. He knew how to learn from his mistakes and was patient, a virtue sadly lacking in many of his contemporaries. Unlike Hideyoshi he never outreached himself. Whereas Hideyoshi ordered a war against China and Korea Ieyasu re-established diplomatic relations with both countries, although Ieyasu's later years were to see Japan's only act of acquisition of overseas territory when the Shimazu invaded the Ryukyu Islands (modern Okinawa Prefecture) on the shogun's behalf. It was to be Ieyasu's grandson the third Tokugawa shogun Iemitsu who closed Japan off from much of the outside world. By contrast, under Ieyasu and Hidetada overseas voyages increased and took in Siam and Cambodia, demonstrating the international outlook of the first two Tokugawa shoguns. It was an open attitude that had one blind spot, and that was Christianity. Ieyasu shared the fears of

Throughout samurai history the best proof of duty done was the presentation of one's enemy's severed head to one's lord. In this detail from a modern painted screen in the Sekigahara Warland Museum we see two of Ieyasu's footsoldiers collecting the haul from the battlefield of Sekigahara.

his predecessor over the likelihood that Christian daimyo might form alliances with countries like Spain, whose activities in East Asia were well known to him, so the Japanese church was persecuted and eventually driven underground.

The suppression of Christianity through the policing of society by the Buddhist clergy and the encouragement of Confucian ideals among the samurai class were the two strands of socio-religious control that Ieyasu's successors were to embrace, and in terms of ensuring their hegemony they succeeded. To establish his family as the ruling clan in Japan for the next two and a half centuries was abundant proof of Ieyasu's greatness, and that was first of all realized through his military achievement as Japan's most successful commander.

WHEN WAR IS DONE

When the dust settled after Sekigahara the retributions began. For example, throughout the whole of the Tohoku Sekigahara campaign Uesugi Kagekatsu, the great northern daimyo on whose behalf the campaign had been waged, had never left the safety of his fortress. His followers had done all the fighting, but if Kagekatsu thought that this would soften the blow he was much mistaken. Ieyasu deprived him of Aizu-Wakamatsu Castle and he saw his fief greatly reduced in size, with its main castle becoming Yonezawa, where the brave *hatamoto* Naoe Kanetsugu had been based. Naoe Kanetsugu continued to serve Uesugi Kagekatsu after the latter pledged allegiance to Ieyasu, and was with him during the Winter Campaign of Osaka, where several daimyo like Kagekatsu were required to prove their worth.

Naoe Kanetsugu's experience was to be typical of many daimyo after Sekigahara, but others were not so lucky. Ishida Mitsunari and Konishi Yukinaga were executed, but although the supreme position which the Tokugawa family were to hold for two and a half centuries had been won on the battlefield, Tokugawa Ieyasu knew that much more than the continued threat of military force was needed if he was to keep Japan from sliding back into a situation of strife that would threaten not only the peace and prosperity of the nation, but also the very survival of his own family. The means by which he did this were far-reaching and complex, and two vast and inter-related initiatives came together to make up the overall pattern of Tokugawa government. Both involved the principle of balance, and both existed within an unquestioned hierarchical framework based on Confucian ideals that saw the shogun at the apex of a harmonious pyramid of authority and duty. The first initiative was known as the *bakuhan* system, whereby a point of equilibrium was found between the central government of the shogun, the *bakufu*, and the decentralized daimyo domains or *han*. The word *bakufu* has the meaning of 'government from behind the curtain', the curtain in question being the field curtains (*maku*) that concealed from prying eyes the headquarters position occupied by a general on the medieval field of battle.

The *han* were the geographical areas, sometimes whole provinces but more often parts of provinces or scattered patchworks of rice fields and villages, that made up the land holdings of the daimyo. To the Tokugawa there were three sorts of daimyo: the *kamon* (the shogun's kinsmen), the *fudai* (the Tokugawa family's hereditary retainers) and the *tozama* (the 'outer lords') who had either been on the losing side at Sekigahara or who had hedged their bets.

The central government of the shogun and the local government of the daimyo therefore existed in a state of blissful Confucian harmony, but to ensure that this blessed situation continued Ieyasu set in motion a redistribution of domains on a grand scale. Over the period of a few years almost all the daimyo of Japan were moved about as if they were so many potted plants, so that ancestral lands and family temples going back centuries were abandoned for distant lands where the nature of the soil, the climate and even the accent of the local inhabitants was totally different. Such a relocation of territory was of itself nothing new. It could come about as a reward for good service, but it could also be used as a punishment. What Tokugawa Ieyasu did was to use relocation for strategic and political purposes, so that the loyal *fudai* received territories from where they could police the activities of the *tozama*, whose links with ancestral support were now thoroughly severed.

A daimyo under the Tokugawa definition controlled a *han* with a value of not less than 10,000 *koku* of rice. (One *koku* was the amount regarded as necessary to feed one man for one year). Below them, at between 100 and 9,500 *koku* were the men now called the *hatamoto*. They were entitled to at least one audience with the shogun. Below the *hatamoto* were the *yoriki* who commanded the 'line infantry' squads of *doshin* or *ashigaru* (foot soldiers) within the Tokugawa army.

Tokugawa Ieyasu is buried on a hill behind one of the world's most spectacular mausoleums – the Great Shrine of Nikko, a Japanese Shinto shrine built ornately in the Chinese style with colour and gold leaf. This is the sacred bridge that leads to the shrine.

A LIFE IN WORDS

Ieyasu left behind a legacy to his successors in the form of written guidance for their behaviour. Called the *Buke Shohatto* it comprises a considerable amount of information both civil and military, such as the symbolic use of the Japanese sword and his cautions against unwise marriage contracts. It begins with a clear statement of Ieyasu's belief in the wisdom of government based on Confucian principles where everyone knows his place in the great hierarchy of harmony. Yet it is very telling that Ieyasu begins by delineating the responsibilities of a ruler to show benevolence to his people rather than the responsibilities of the people to show loyalty and obedience to those above them. This principle of *noblesse oblige* is often forgotten in the usual assumptions made about the absolute rule of the samurai class. Military matters appear very early in the document, and here Ieyasu reflects the views of the great Ancient Chinese strategist Son Zi (Sun Tzu) who believed in the economy of forces and the advisability of achieving political ends without war if this was possible. So Ieyasu writes, 'The right use of a sword is that it should subdue the barbarians while lying gleaming in its scabbard. If it leaves the sheath it cannot be said to be used rightly. Similarly the right use of military power is that it should conquer the enemy while concealed in the breast.'

But this threat of force must be backed up by genuine prowess: 'A warrior who does not understand the Way of the Warrior and the samurai who does not know the principles of the samurai can only be called a stupid or petty general, by no means a good one.'

His most famous comment, 'The sword is the soul of the warrior. If any forget or lose it he will not be excused,' follows shortly after.

In this middle section of a three-panel print Tokugawa Ieyasu sits surrounded by some of his most loyal generals. Honda Tadakatsu with his antler helmet sits at his lord's right front.

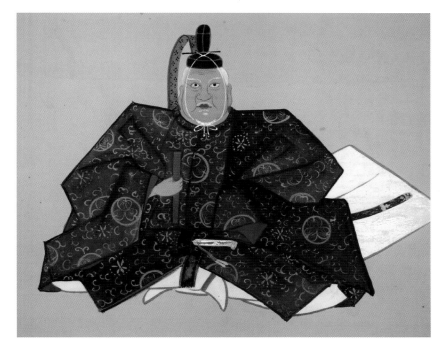

Tokugawa Ieyasu is shown as the elder statesman of the Tokugawa family in this painted scroll in the Sekigahara Warland Museum. Ieyasu retired from the position of shogun in 1605 in favour of his son Hidetada but continued to exert great influence behind the scenes until his death in 1616.

Somewhat strangely, there are far fewer pictorial sources for the life of Ieyasu than there are for his predecessor Toyotomi Hideyoshi. As Ieyasu's successors were ruling as shoguns during the early 19th century it was considered insulting to reproduce images of their illustrious predecessor in the newly fashionable genre of the woodblock print or the illustrated book. So whereas Hideyoshi's life is meticulously illustrated in such works as *Ehon Taikoki*, woodblock pictures of Ieyasu are quite rare until the time of the Meiji Restoration.

FURTHER READING AND PLACES TO VISIT

The classic biography of Tokugawa Ieyasu is A. L. Sadler's *The Maker of Modern Japan* of 1937, recently republished in paperback by Tuttle and Co. under the new title of S*hogun: The Life of Tokugawa Ieyasu*. *Tokugawa Ieyasu Shogun* is also the title of a biography of Ieyasu by Conrad Totman (1983). In Japanese, several volumes in the *Rekishi Gunzo* series cover Ieyasu. These include *Tokugawa Ieyasu, Sekigahara no tatakai, Ishida Mitsunari* and *Tokugawa Ieyasu Shitenno*. The campaign of Osaka is covered in detail in my Osprey Campaign volume *Osaka 1615* (2006). For those who can read Japanese it may be pointed out that a novel based on the life of Tokugawa Ieyasu appears in the Guinness Book of Records as the world's longest novel!

The memory of Japan's great shogun is well preserved in Japan. Pride of place goes to Ieyasu's last resting place in Nikko, where his mausoleum lies in a beautiful wooded area within an ornate Chinese-style Shinto shrine. The Toshogu, as it is called, is one of the great sights of Japan, and its festivals involving *yabusame* (horseback archery) as an offering to Ieyasu's spirit are justly celebrated. His former castles of Hamamatsu and Okazaki contain much of interest and Shizuoka, the former Sumpu where he was held hostage as a child, celebrates him every bit as enthusiastically. Near Shizuoka is the Kunozan Toshogu Shrine, which is like a miniature Nikko and contains armour of Ieyasu and the later shoguns. In Tokyo the Imperial Palace, old Edo Castle, is not open to the public, but the vast area around the inner moat, which is a public park, shows how enormous the shogun's capital once was. As to battlefields, Mikatagahara, north of Hamamatsu, is now the city cemetery, but nearby Saigadake has an interesting museum and monuments. The area between Komaki and Nagakute can be traversed in a day on foot, while the strangest site of all is the temple in Sakai called the Nanshuji, where the priest will be delighted to show you the grave of Tokugawa Ieyasu, supposedly killed and substituted for at the battle of Tennoji.

Much more can be gained by a visit to the site of the battle of Sekigahara, which is still an isolated rural area between Maibara (the junction of the Tokaido Shinkansen ('Bullet Train') and Ogaki. The fact that a highway, an expressway, a main line railway and the Shinkansen pass through it has served to preserve the main features rather than destroy them. Sekigahara has its own station (served only by local stopping trains), and just to the north of the railway line lies the Sekigahara Museum, an excellent place recently completely refurbished with videos, models, quite a lot of genuine arms and armour, and some very good reproduction costumes and flags of the main protagonists. Maps and guides in English to the battlefield are readily available, and there are several way-marked paths round the sites which cover an extensive area. Each is easy to find because of the daimyo's banners that fly there. Ishida Mitsunari's campsite sits prominently on a nearby hill, but a car is needed to visit Kobayakawa's post on Matsuoyama. There is also Sekigahara Warland, which has seen better days. It has a small museum with two very good reproduction painted screens of the battle but also the rather dilapidated set of rather sweet concrete dummies that represent key moments in the battle. They are out in the open air and have suffered from the weather.

GLOSSARY

Ashigaru	foot soldiers, under the Tokugawa the lowest ranks of the samurai class
Bakufu	the shogunate, 'government within the curtain'
Bakuhan	the system of balance between the shogun and the daimyo under the Tokugawa

Bodaji	family temple
Bugyo	magistrates or civil officials; in an army the General Staff
Bun and Bu	the civil and the military arts as accomplishments of a samurai.
Daimyo	independent warlord, later feudal lord under the Tokugawa regime
Doshin	foot soldiers under the Tokugawa
Fudai	inner lords, hereditary retainers of the Tokugawa
Gembuku	manhood ceremony
Go	a board game of strategy
Gundan	war band, the vassals from whom a daimyo's army would be formed
Han	a daimyo's domain under the shogun
Hatamoto	the closest bodyguard to the Shogun, literally 'under the standard'
Ikki	leagues, also riots caused by leagues
Jinbaori	surcoat
Jinya	a temporary fortified military encampment
Kagemusha	a look-like substitute for a general, literally 'shadow warrior'
Kakemono	hanging scroll
Kami	a deity in the religion of Shinto
Kamon	the shogun's kinsmen
Karo	elder or senior vassal who would act in the daimyo's absence
Maedate	helmet frontlet/crest
Maku	the curtains that enclosed a general's field headquarters
Mon	a family badge or crest
Ninja	an undercover agent or warrior
Nobori	long banner
Ronin	a masterless samurai, 'man of the waves'
Samurai	a Japanese knight, a member of the military aristocracy
Shogi	Japanese chess
Shogun	the military dictator of Japan
Taisho	general
Tozama	'outer lords' who submitted to Ieyasu only after being defeated by him or after witnessing his triumph
Yabusame	horseback archery
Yoriki	leaders of foot soldiers

INDEX